Christian Life and Witness

Princeton Theological Monograph Series

K. C. Hanson, Charles M. Collier, and D. Christopher Spinks,
Series Editors

Recent volumes in the series:

Linda Hogan and Dylan Lehrke, editors
Religion and Politics of Peace and Conflict

Chris Budden
Following Jesus in Invaded Space: Doing Theology on Aboriginal Land

Ryan A. Neal
*Theology as Hope: On the Ground and Implications of
Jürgen Moltmann's Doctrine of Hope*

David Hein
Geoffrey Fisher: Archbishop of Canterbury, 1945–1961

Catherine L. Kelsey
*Schleiermacher's Preaching, Dogmatics, and Biblical Criticism:
The Interpretation of Jesus Christ in the Gospel of John*

Christian T. Collins Winn
*"Jesus Is Victor!": The Significance of the Blumhardts
for the Theology of Karl Barth*

Abraham Kunnuthara
Schleiermacher on Christian Consciousness of God's Work in History

Paul S. Chung
Martin Luther and Buddhism: Aesthetics of Suffering, Second Edition

Philip Ruge-Jones
*Cross in Tensions: Luther's Theology of the Cross
as Theologico-social Critique*

Jedediah Mannis
Joseph Tuckerman and the Outdoor Church

Jerry Root
C. S. Lewis and a Problem of Evil: An Investigation of a Pervasive Theme

Eliseo Pérez-Álvarez
A Vexing Gadfly: The Late Kierkegaard on Economic Matters

Christian Life and Witness

Count Zinzendorf's 1738 Berlin Speeches

NIKOLAUS LUDWIG VON ZINZENDORF

Edited, translated, and with an introduction and notes by
Gary S. Kinkel

PICKWICK *Publications* · Eugene, Oregon

CHRISTIAN LIFE AND WITNESS
Count Zinzendorf's 1738 Berlin Speeches

Princeton Theological Monograph Series 140

Pickwick Publications
An Imprint of Wipf and Stock Publishers
199 W. 8th Ave., Suite 3
Eugene, OR 97401

www.wipfandstock.com

ISBN 13: 978-1-60608-617-9

Cataloging-in-Publication data:

Zinzendorf, Nikolaus Ludwig Graf von, 1700–1760.

Christian life and witness : Count Zinzendorf's 1738 Berlin speeches / Nikolaus Ludwig von Zinzendorf; edited, translated and with an introduction and notes by Gary S. Kinkel.

ISBN 13: 978-1-60608-617-9

Princeton Theological Monograph Series 140

xxvi + 138 p. ; 23 cm.—Includes bibliographical references.

1. Zinzendorf, Nikolaus Ludwig Graf von, 1700–1760—Sources. 2. Zinzendorf, Nikolaus Ludwig Graf von, 1700–1760—Theology. 3. Bohemian Brethren. I. Kinkel, Gary S. II. Title. III. Series.

BX4820 Z5 2010

Manufactured in the U.S.A.

Contents

Acknowledgments

I HAVE BEEN HELPED BY A NUMBER OF PEOPLE IN THE PREPARATION OF these pages. I owe thanks to Dr. Patricia Caulkins, professor of German at Simpson College, Indianola, Iowa, for her patient examination of the translation. All awkward constructions are my own, of course, but this work would not be nearly as good without her input. I owe thanks, as well, to my children, Nikolas, Monika, and Madeline for pushing me with their questions, their enthusiasms, and their pure excitement about life, justice, and hope. And finally, I owe a great debt of thanks to my wife, Kay, who encouraged me, prayed for me, and loved me through thick and thin as this book moved toward completion.

Gary S. Kinkel
Indianola, Iowa

Translator's Introduction

NIKOLAUS LUDWIG COUNT VON ZINZENDORF CAME INTO THE WORLD on May 26, 1700, in the German city of Dresden. He died in Herrnhut on May 9, 1760. His life was filled with both controversy and paradox. He was a theologian who never formally studied theology. In an age of harsh literary and institutional battles between Lutheran Orthodoxy and Pietism, he grew up in a family intimately associated with the leading figures of Lutheran Pietism, yet earned his degree at Wittenberg University, the great fortress of Lutheran Orthodoxy. As a young man, his Christian convictions drove him to embrace pacifism, but he was employed by the government as special counsel to the king of Saxony. He was a representative of the law who conducted illegal religious meetings in his Dresden apartment and wrote and printed anonymously (on his own press) a totally illegal, critical, religious periodical under the pen name "the Dresden Socrates." He was a member of the high nobility, a relative and friend of kings, who spent a good deal of his adult life in close association with uneducated laborers, religious dissenters, black slaves from the West Indies, and native people in America. He was a devoted follower of Luther who carried on a deep personal friendship with a Roman Catholic cardinal during the days when Lutherans and Catholics regarded each other with open hostility. He was a lover of the Lutheran confessional documents who opened his heart and even his house and lands to religious radicals and dissenters who confessed Jesus Christ but ignored the Lutheran confessions and rejected the state church structure. There were Mennonite preachers who spoke highly of him, while some of his fellow Lutherans considered him mad. A highly cultured intellectual who was engaged with, and appreciative of, much of the Enlightenment, a lover particularly of the work of the philosopher Pierre Bayle, he lived by a simple, passionate, and profound faith in Jesus, the Lamb of God. In an age when most Christians in Europe and the Americas heaped abuse and contempt upon Jews and Judaism, he befriended Jews and learned from them. Indeed, he began to use Yiddish expressions in his speech. Though accused of being a "quietist," it is hard to imagine anyone more dynamic, engaged, and unquiet.

For all that, one might be tempted to dismiss him as a historically interesting character, but certainly not someone who might bear meaningful theological fruit in the present. Such a conclusion would be badly mistaken. Count Zinzendorf has had, and continues to have, an influence that compels further study and engagement with him. He ought to be read and considered, if for no other reason, for the significance of the people who have been profoundly shaped and influenced by him. He was without question the most influential German theologian between Luther and Schleiermacher. He was a decisive influence on both Schleiermacher and Kierkegaard. He stood behind much of the preaching of Johann Christoph Blumhardt. In the twentieth century Karl Barth came to praise him. Jürgen Moltmann dedicated one of his books to the spiritual heirs of Zinzendorf. Dietrich Bonhoeffer, too, bears the imprint of Zinzendorf. But in order to catch a glimpse of how he might relate to the present, it is necessary to understand him first in his own time and context. In this short essay I will suggest some of the significant features of the age in which he lived, sketch the course of his own life, and, finally, point to a few reasons he ought to continue to matter to Christians even in the present.

The time of Zinzendorf's birth in Dresden as the son of an imperial count was an age of cultural flowering in Saxony. It was a high-water mark for the region. Art, literature, and language were shaped by the style called "baroque." It is not too much to say that Dresden was, in fact, a center of baroque culture. In other words, paintings, buildings, sculpture, and speech were ornately decorated. There were gratuitous flourishes everywhere. If a painting seemed to require excessive ornament, then in speech a simple declarative sentence could hardly do. The reader will encounter in Zinzendorf this baroque inclination to speak prose as if it were poetry; to construct long sentences with subordinate clauses; to say, not merely "God," but "the dear, kind God;" to say not merely "Jesus," but to add a whole parenthetical list of titles. It is language with a flourish.

Politically, it was the age of absolutism in Saxony, following the French model. The electoral prince of Saxony, or elector, was Friedrich August I (1670–1733), called "the Strong." In 1697 he took the Polish throne, and in Poland his title was "August II." Thus, from 1697–1733 he ruled both Saxony and Poland. He was continually in need of money, not least because he spent extravagantly. But extravagant spending seemed to fit the baroque spirit. He had grand, one might say fantastic, political plans. His faith, his relation to God, was decidedly secondary to and in the service of, his political ambitions. It was this, together with his absolutist program, which provoked criticism and opposition from the ranks of the Saxon nobility.

A movement had taken shape and gained momentum among the nobility, some professors of theology, and some clergy. A good deal of the criticism of the prince came from people active in this movement who were particularly moved to opposition by the prince's willingness to sacrifice faith for political ends. The movement came to be called "Pietism." A number of sources gave rise to it. But Lutheran Pietism had one central conviction: that Lutheran theology, the Lutheran confessional writings, worship attendance, talk about God, indeed, the very existence of the Christian Church itself, amounted to emptiness, at best a thin ethical porridge and some metaphysical crumbs, apart from living faith in Jesus Christ that is active in love, a deep personal engagement with Scripture, and a life of prayer. Pietists reacted strongly against a Christianity that had come to be indentified largely with the cognitive: getting the doctrine right. While they did not disparage right doctrine, they called for a Christian life that likewise engaged the affective, the volitional, and the ethical. With the doctrine as a framework a Christian life must be constructed, they thought, by a vital relationship of trust and love with the One to whom all the doctrines point and bear witness; and this relationship, if it is authentic, must shape and drive the affections, the will, and the way one conducted oneself.

The Pietist interest in the will and the affections drove them to a close acquaintance with devotional literature and intense engagement with the Bible. They also learned to open themselves to each other and to speak the truth to each other even when it was hard. But their attention was not turned merely to the inward. Lutheran Pietists had begun sending missionaries outside the continent to take the message concerning Jesus Christ to people who had not heard it. These missionaries were few and the sending was sporadic, but they were the first Protestant missionaries sent to foreign lands.

Lutheran Orthodox theologians sharply opposed the Pietist movement. They accused Pietists of altering doctrine, of subjectivizing the objective truths of the faith, of putting all the emphasis on regeneration and renewal rather than on justification, of thinking and speaking of salvation in a synergistic way (i.e., as though God's grace does not accomplish all, but rather requires our action), of undermining the status and function of the clergy, and of embarking on mission when God had not called for it. Orthodoxy argued that the Gospel had already been carried to every place God intended it to go. Therefore, there was to be no mission. If there were people who had never had an opportunity to hear the Gospel, to hear of Jesus Christ, it was the fault of their ancestors, who presumably had rejected the message. Pietism continued on its way nevertheless. There were exchanges, sometimes harsh, between Lutheran Orthodox and Lutheran Pietist leaders.

Among the Pietist critics of Friedrich August the Strong was one of the prince's own counselors, an imperial count named Georg Ludwig von Zinzendorf. Georg Ludwig was a close friend of Philipp Jakob Spener, who is usually referred to as the founder of the Lutheran Pietist movement. Moreover, Georg Ludwig von Zinzendorf was the father of Nikolaus Ludwig, the author of our speeches.

Six weeks after Nikolaus was born Georg Ludwig, 38 years old, died of what seems to have been tuberculosis. Nikolaus' mother, Charlotte Justine (daughter of Nikolaus von Gersdorf, prefect of Upper Lusatia) took her infant son and went to live with her parents. Two older children from Georg Ludwig's first marriage went to live with Georg Ludwig's brother, a Field Marshall. Two years later Nikolaus von Gersdorf himself died. At that point, Charlotte's mother moved the whole family to her ancestral home, the castle of Gross Hennersdorf in Upper Lusatia, roughly sixty miles east of Dresden. In 1704 Charlotte married Dubislaw Gneomer von Natzmer, a Prussian Field Marshall, and moved with him to Berlin. Four-year-old Nikolaus was left with his grandmother in Gross Hennersdorf.

All this leaving behind of children following death and remarriage may strike the contemporary reader as very strange, or at least very sad. But this is how life was in eighteenth century Europe. Death often came early and children had to be taken in by relatives or friends. It was

Nikolaus' great good fortune to be left to be nurtured and educated by his grandmother, Henriette Katherina von Gersdorf.

Henriette Katherina von Gersdorf was a brilliant and accomplished woman. She had gained recognition among the educated as a poet in both German and Latin. She painted in oils and was a talented musician. By letter from her castle she continued to wield considerable influence at Friedrich August the Strong's court in Dresden. Moreover, she corresponded with Leibniz, the great German philosopher. She read his work and engaged his thought critically. His letters to her reveal that he took her very seriously as a philosophical conversation partner. Long before Nikolaus' birth she had been an enthusiastic participant in the Lutheran Pietist movement. There were Pietist gatherings in her castle and Pietist leaders such as Philipp Spener, August Hermann Francke, and Paul Anton were frequent guests in her home. She made generous financial contributions to their projects (e.g., the Franckesche Stiftung, which is still in operation today in the city of Halle and was founded and built partly with von Gersdorf money). She took care of large numbers of orphans, widows, and the poor in her region. She read theology in both German and Latin and learned biblical Hebrew and Koine Greek in order to read the Scriptures in their original languages. Finally, she managed the large estate that came with her castle with dexterity and skill. So it was to this powerful and remarkable woman that Zinzendorf's mother entrusted his care. Nor did it do any harm that little Nikolaus was the apple of her eye.

There were no other small children on this (then) somewhat remote estate. So the Count grew up without playmates his own age. He spent a considerable amount of time during his childhood alone, though his mother's sister still lived in the castle. She was fifteen years older than he and was more like another parent than a playmate. Still, during his childhood their relationship was close.

Zinzendorf participated daily in the devotional services his grandmother led, attendance at which was required for all the employees of the estate. He was sometimes underfoot in the midst of the estate's bustling activity. But he also made his own projects. And his grandmother von Gersdorf undertook his education. Some of it was carried out by hired tutors and some of it she did herself. But his engagement with other people was with adults and not with other children.

In the midst of all this activity—particularly the Scripture, prayer, and hymns of the devotional exercises, with famous Pietist leaders coming and going—it is not surprising that this extraordinarily talented child was also religiously precocious. There are many stories of his seeking ways to express his love for Jesus. As a very small boy he wrote notes to Jesus, expressing his devotion to and love for his Savior. He would throw the notes out the window so that the Savior would receive them. After public worship he could repeat the pastor's prayers verbatim for the adults.

In 1706 Swedish armies under Charles XII overran Saxony. A military unit appeared on the estate to commandeer supplies. Entering the castle intent upon ransacking it they burst into a room in which the then six-year-old Zinzendorf was carrying on his usual private devotions. The Swedish soldiers were, like the little count, Lutherans. They paused in their assignment to listen to him speak about Jesus Christ, and to pray with him!

As an adult he said he had never known a time when he did not love the Savior above all things. He experienced no conversion, no hard won repentance, no turning from a dissolute life or from casual indifference to the cross. From his earliest consciousness he lived by faith in the Savior who loved him and gave himself up for him. Always, the Lamb of God, slaughtered on the cross, was central to his cognitive, affective, volitional, and practical life.

In addition to training him in the Christian life, his grandmother also impressed upon him continually that he was born a *Reichsgraf,* a member of the upper nobility along with princes, electors, and the emperor himself. She taught him that God had given him such a high and noble birth and he must use it to rule. Thus, his education was directed to preparing him to govern. He learned languages (he was polylinguistic all his life), history, geography, mathematics and a host of social skills so that he might be able to carry himself properly. She also believed that rulers must conduct themselves with great discipline. So he was also trained to have great self-discipline, great self-control. By all accounts this self-discipline came with difficulty for him. He had a passionate nature. And despite all this training for government, Zinzendorf wrote many years later that his grandmother's education had shaped him in such a way that he could relish nothing except the doctrine of Jesus Christ and his death and merit.

When it was time for him to prepare to attend a university, it should come as no surprise that his grandmother sent him as a boarder to the prep school operated by her friend, the Pietist leader and educator August Hermann Francke. Thus, he travelled to Halle in August of 1710 to study. His teachers and fellow students made his life a trial. They conspired to make him miserable. The reason behind his harsh treatment lay in a letter Zinzendorf's mother had sent to Francke. Since her son was clearly a boy of great ability, she urged Francke to break his spirit and keep him down in order that pride not take root in his heart. He also had to endure simultaneously a tutor who clearly disliked Zinzendorf and tried both directly and deviously to destroy his reputation and to get him removed from the school. But the circumstances revealed that the boy had great inner resources and relied on his Savior. He not only survived the ordeal, but when he left at the age of sixteen to matriculate at university he turned over to Francke a list of seven groups of boys, all of which he had started, and with all of which he met. Each of these groups would meet at its appointed time, apart from adults in some secluded place, and Zinzendorf would lead them in prayer, in sharing the true state of their hearts, and in learning to refer all things in their lives to the Savior who loved them.

While taking his leave from Halle, Count Zinzendorf prayed with one of his close friends, a Swiss noble named de Watteville. The two sixteen-year-olds pledged that they each would do all in their power to carry the message concerning Jesus Christ to all people, but especially to those to whom no one else would go, or about whom no one else cared. This pledge would later be carried out in astounding fashion.

It was decided that he would attend the University of Wittenberg. It was the place where Luther had been professor of Bible two hundred years earlier, and it was, in Zinzendorf's day, one of the leading institutions of Lutheran Orthodoxy. It was also decided that he would study law. At that time, such decisions were not made by the student. The family, most particularly his parents and his grandmother, made these decisions for him.

In Wittenberg he continued with a tutor who did not understand, and who was totally unsympathetic to his religious life. The tutor had been hired by his father's brother, who was deeply opposed to Pietism. Nevertheless, the sixteen-year-old set himself a rigorous devotional program. He also took to handing out Pietist tracts on the streets of this city whose university was the very bastion of Orthodoxy. Although he was supposed to be study law, he snuck into lectures in theology. He was befriended by a professor of theology who took him under his wing and guided his theological reading. Many years later the count remarked that what he really learned at Wittenberg was not law, but theology. And the theology he learned was that of Lutheran Orthodoxy.

While still a teen he undertook to bring the leaders of Orthodoxy and Pietism together for formal discussions. His intention was to bring about rapprochement. He had personal contacts with both sides and viewed this as a call from God to make peace between them. He had gone as far as arranging a meeting when his family intervened and de-railed the project. In their view he was only a student, and not even a theology student, therefore he was meddling in matters that were not his affair. His family ordered him to withdraw. As a result, the meeting never happened, and Orthodoxy and Pietism continued in their sharp opposition to each other.

Upon completing his degree in law, Zinzendorf was sent on a trip around Europe. This was considered a necessary part of a young noble's education. On this trip he was to build an international network of friends and acquaintances, looking forward to the day when he would wield power, and to become more finely cultured by seeing the great art, architecture, and historical sites of the continent. Zinzendorf spent much of his time seeking friends who shared his love for Jesus and en-gaging in deep conversations with those who did not. He wanted to talk about the Scriptures rather than governing.

He met Christians who represented theological perspectives other than his own Lutheran one. And even if he disagreed with them about some points of doctrine, he found that they were united in their devo-tion to the Savior and his grace. This seemed important to him, espe-cially in view of the rise of theoretical atheism, which he increasingly encountered. So, contrary to what was thought properly Christian by all sides, he began to cultivate close relationships with Christians who were not Lutheran. Among these were a Catholic Cardinal in Paris and the future British governor of the colony of Georgia.

Although he was forthright about his desire to preach the Gospel, his grandmother reminded him that he was an imperial count. Imperial counts did not preach; they exercised their office and ruled. So, through her connections at court, she got him a position as special counsel to

Friedrich August the Strong—the same position his father had held with the same prince. In 1722 he rented an apartment in Dresden and took up his new post. With great energy he promptly set himself to the task of avoiding actual government work as much as possible. He was surrounded by ambitious men who were eager to take on the cases that were originally given to him.

Feeling himself compelled by the words and way of Jesus to reject war, weapons, and all forms of violence, he nevertheless worked for the state. Thus, Zinzendorf walked the hallways engaging in conversation about Jesus with both colleagues and visitors. It must have been strange for many who came into the halls of power for state purposes to encounter this young count asking them questions like, "So then, how do you understand the Savior's word to love our enemies?" But such questions he incessantly asked.

He also held illegal religious meetings in his apartments. He would lead the gathered company in devotions and engage in theological argument with non-Lutherans.

During this period he also acquired a printing press. There were strict laws governing publishing. In particular, all printed matter had to pass a government censor who represented the interests of both the state church and the government. The censor was one of Zinzendorf's colleagues, occupying an office not far from Zinzendorf's own. The Count used his press to write, publish, and distribute a weekly underground paper, which he called *The Dresden Socrates*. He did it all anonymously, of course. In this paper he was critical of the church and of the religious life of the people, and he raised probing questions about both. Meanwhile, the government embarked on a furious search for the author and distributor of this illegal publication, never discovering that he was one of them.

It was also during this period, in September of 1722, that he married Erdmuth Dorothea, Countess Reuss. The Countess was known for her piety and devotion. He judged that she would make a good partner for him. At the beginning of their marriage he turned all financial affairs over to her. It was highly unusual in the eighteenth century for a woman to be in charge of finances. But it seemed even more radical when, in 1732, he gave her legal title to all his property (thereby making her the owner and not himself).

It was also in 1722 that a band of ten religious refugees appeared on Zinzendorf's estate. The Count approved their staying on his lands until a more permanent place could be found for them. He seems to have intended that they should eventually have moved to the lands of his father-in-law, Count Reuss, a Pietist who was already sheltering some religious dissenters. But this never happened. Instead, with the Count's approval from Dresden, they began to build a small settlement on Zinzendorf's lands.

This community came to be called *Herrnhut* (the Lord's watch). It began to attract religious dissenters of different kinds. Such people heard there was a place where they could live free of persecution. The story of the development of this community and of Zinzendorf's engagement with and influence upon them is interesting in itself. Suffice it to say here, that the community became the vehicle for Zinzendorf's adolescent pledge to preach the Gospel to every creature, and especially to those for whom no one else cared. After a stunning experience of the power and grace of God, this little community became an intrepid, irresistible legion of missionaries undaunted by disease, distance, risk, or death. And die they did, only to be replaced by new volunteers who joyously went to carry the news of the Savior. Within a decade this community of three hundred people had missionaries on every inhabited continent. True to Zinzendorf's youthful promise, they went first to those places and peoples to whom no one else would go because the journey, the environment, or the people themselves were too dangerous. Moreover, these missionaries, lacking any theological training, were extraordinarily effective.

Zinzendorf led the missionary effort and at the same time continued his engagement with the churches in Europe. He formed a society within the churches that transcended the boundaries of the confessions. His aim was to bring together those whose hearts were bound to the Savior through love. Some further communities modeled on *Herrnhut* were also formed. They constituted a renewal of the pre-Reformation Hussite church from Bohemia and Moravia. They quickly came to be called the "Moravian Brethren" or the "Moravian Church." The intention was not to be a church alongside other churches. Rather, in Zinzendorf's conception they were to be a fellowship, a leaven, within all the churches, calling people to the heart of the Gospel, to a response to God's love in Jesus Christ that was passionately loving, and to a resulting love for people of all kinds, including and especially the excluded, the overlooked, and the neglected. Within Europe this produced concern for and activity on behalf of prisoners, the mentally ill, and the developmentally challenged.

The Count seemed to be everywhere. His customary practice was to speak extemporaneously. Much of the material in his *Hauptschriften* (major writings) consists of transcripts of speeches given on various occasions for different purposes. His appearances, his speeches, the missionary activity, the trans-confessional societies, and his way of using language all provoked heated opposition from the Orthodox (with some exceptions, e.g., the theological faculty at Tübingen supported him) and from other Pietists. Nevertheless, he carried on. The speeches contained in the present volume come from the mature Zinzendorf. He gave them in Berlin at almost the midpoint of his adult life. His aim was to clarify the main point, the central point, of Christian life. He intended to do that by commenting on Luther's explication of the second article of the creed, the one dealing with Jesus Christ.

What did his thought contribute to the wider Christian community? First, the explosion into the world of those missionaries from *Herrnhut* and its related communities gave birth to modern Protestant missions. Subsequent missionary movements, and missionaries, were inspired and informed by this Zinzendorf and his *Herrnhuters*.

Second, his effort to unite Christians across confessional boundaries on the basis of Jesus Christ himself was the impulse and idea that gave rise to the ecumenical movement. Some began to take his talk seriously. Moving along the trajectory of his language and thought, they pushed discussions of the meaning of the divisions between Christians, and the meaning of Christian community and Christian faith, in such a direction that two centuries later brought the ecumenical movement into being. Paradoxically, against his intention, this effort also brought the Lutheran Church in America into being. His idea of forming one Christian church in which each of the theological and liturgical traditions would remain and have their own integrity seemed very dangerous to his contemporaries. Thus, when he travelled to North America, Lutheran authorities in Germany who had before that time mostly ignored requests from America for a Lutheran pastor, immediately sent Muhlenberg to organize the Lutherans in America as a distinct and separate church, and to wrest them away from Zinzendorf's influence.

Third, he was a prolific writer of hymn texts and had a great impact on Western Christian hymnody. Under his direction the Moravian Fellowship was a musical band of missionaries.

Fourth, in days when the great storm of the Reformation seemed to have burned down to a few coals, he called for faith to become again a living, blazing fire rather than a cold acceptance of doctrinal formulations and a formal adherence to socially accepted manners and morality.

Of great significance was his engagement with the Enlightenment. This was many sided. There were features of that intellectual movement that he regarded as good and some that he rejected quite forcefully. He was in agreement, for theological reasons, with the Enlightenment's call for religious toleration. Indeed, he preferred people who were passionate about and deeply devoted to what they regarded as holy to those who were casual or indifferent or, as he put it, "cold minded." In contrast to many of his Christian contemporaries, he embraced biblical criticism. Anything that helps us better understand the texts that preach Christ to us was a good thing in his estimation. Thus, while many Christians feared and attacked early scholarly forays into historical criticism, Zinzendorf welcomed them as useful.

Also, he loved the philosophical writings of Pierre Bayle, who is sometimes called the grandfather of the Enlightenment. He particularly loved Bayle's merciless criticism of every human system, every intellectual pretense, and every confident claim to knowledge. He loved Bayle's demand for plain speech and his refusal to whitewash matters either ethical or religious.

Moreover, most, if not all, other Christian thinkers of the period engaged Enlightenment deism and atheism by trying to argue within the terms and limits set by Enlightenment thinkers. Christians accepted from these Enlightenment thinkers, mostly without criticism, how God was to be spoken of and argued for, i.e., what conceptual scheme was acceptable. They accepted the Enlightenment understanding of reason and the Enlightenment's meaning or use of the term "truth." Thus, the game was lost before it was even begun. But in stark contrast, Zinzendorf sharply rejected these. He refused to play on a field marked out by the Enlightenment and doubted they were even playing the same game. Central to this was his refusal to accept or engage in any talk about God that was not talk about Jesus. God as a cold abstraction, as the conclusion arrived at by a chain of human reasoning or observation of the world, as something or someone whose being and purposes could be somehow sketched out by rationality was for Zinzendorf nothing but a *chimera* (his word) concocted out of human desires and wishes and shaped by the limits of reason. It reflected nothing more than the limits themselves. Concepts of "God" resulting from reason and observation were nothing more than the mirror of finitude. They were not concepts of the real God. God could only be spoken of on the basis of God's own act and God's own speech: Jesus Christ.

Zinzendorf was thus radically christocentric. For him, no Scripture passage is really rightly understood until it has been referred to Jesus Christ. No statement about God can be taken seriously with respect to truth unless it is about and one way or another has reference to Jesus Christ. No talk about what a Christian ought to do or how one ought to navigate the world is legitimate unless it is about and has direct reference to Jesus Christ. In an age that began to be squeamish about reference to God, he boldly spoke a full and rich Trinitarian God and did not hesitate to refer to Jesus as "God incarnate." At the same time, one would have difficulty locating a Christian thinker who takes more seriously or considers more directly the full and authentic humanity of Jesus. All this is clear in the speeches in this volume.

There are other things interesting and noteworthy in Zinzendorf that warrant more study and discussion. He was working on understanding child development and tried to focus communication for children in ways that were appropriate for them. He had a sense of the systemic character of sin and therefore knew that it is not enough for individual sinners to be justified and saved. God calls forth a new community to live a different way by different forms and to stand over against the "system of sin" as a witness to the presence and grace of God. He unhesitatingly used feminine language for God, specifically for the Holy Spirit. He tried to move beyond trapping God in human categories while recognizing that such forms are the only ones we can use to speak of God.

Of special note, too, is his work for renewal among Christians and his lifelong commitment to evangelism and mission. His commitment to mission was a commitment to do all for the Savior and to call all people into the eschatological community of Jesus. He did not do this because he thought people would be otherwise damned. He did it so that they could know the joy of life in Christ, lived toward resurrection from the dead and the redemption of all things. His commitment was so total that by the time of his death he was broke. All of his great wealth and resources he gave to the mission; every last penny. There are tremendous resources in his thought and in his life for a Christian Church in the twenty-first century that is uncertain, increasingly marginalized, and tempted to abandon discipleship and theology for the sake of making itself attractive. Zinzendorf did not think a good set of management principles would bring about the renewal of life that can be brought only by the living Lord, Jesus Christ.

Finally, the golden thread one can trace through the whole course of his life is his passion for the Savior. His passionate attachment to Jesus never grew dim. It informed everything he did and said. It shines like a nova on every page of these speeches.

The translation that follows is based upon the text contained in Volume I of the Olms edition of the *Hauptschriften* edited by Erich Beyreuther and Gerhard Meyer. This text was an edition of the *Speeches* revised by Zinzendorf and published by Gottfried Clemens in 1758. The full title of the 1758 edition was *Des Ordinarii Fratrum Berlinische Reden, nach dem vollständigen und von ihm selbst eigenhändig revidirten Exemplar*. In the eighteenth century there were two English translations of the *Speeches* and John Wesley published a selection from them. The biblical references are part of the original published text. They may or may not come from Zinzendorf. He did oversee the publication of these speeches, but an editor may have added the references. Zinzendorf always spoke extemporaneously and thus, when he quoted Scripture or any other source, he quoted from memory. I did not use any modern English translation of the Bible for Scripture quotations, but followed Zinzendorf's own iteration of the text.

Zinzendorf's Preface

I HAVE SEEN SEVERAL CONCEPTIONS OF MY SPEECHES FROM GOOD minds, which they no doubt meant really in a Christian way; but it was their words, not mine, and their ideas, not mine, which therefore I have thrown away, not because I held them to be lesser than my own, but rather because first of all they are simply not mine. There are whole speeches in their complete connection that have gone around Berlin under my name, and it struck me that the text, the theme, and the words were simply fabricated.

To be sure, I have endured this with patience, but the circumstances have shown me the necessity to lay before the eyes of everyone at least the basic concepts of all my speeches, apart from which I have spoken nothing essential. Whoever understands a little what they read, sees likewise that I deal with only four matters.

The first is: The essential, one and only, eternal God who became human.

The second: The true, essential, natural and pure humanity of the God of heaven.

The third: That the one way to salvation for all people is that, for the sake of the merit of the slaughtered Lamb, they receive grace and the forgiveness of all their sins and remain his own poor and wretched people in time and eternity.

The fourth: That it is no wonder that to all to whom sin is rightly well known, and who receive permission to sin no more, to give up sin and lead a godly life; that it is only the application of the costly privilege that Jesus expensively purchased for us with his blood, and which no one will relinquish, whose head stands in the right place.

I have sought to place [these four things] in such a light, with the conciseness of the truth in itself, through the simplicity of the recitation, that I believe no person who takes the Bible as God's Word and has as well grasped the most common ideas by thinking and speaking can deny [these four things].

The reason I repeated these four things so often in my speeches was that I didn't have the same listeners every time and I wanted to say something [about these four matters] to each one. But now, the reason [for this publication], is, as I said above, that I wanted to have my speeches as they [actually] were.

With the exception of these discourses over the [second] article, I rarely had texts [to explain]. The first saying [in most cases] was more a beginning of my speech than [an announcement] that I wanted to exegete for my listeners once again the same places of Scripture, after so many explanations of it have been heard and read. When I hear a word from God, then the thoughts or words that belong to it follow all by themselves. It is just like a full barrel when someone takes the cork out of its side. Ah, my Savior, if only I would have the pleasure, that my readers might experience what I experience, and that their hearts might burn when they read a word about Jesus in these pages!

There is only one thing more I can say.

I am verbally attacked in the world in a wholly unusual way. I regard even the least of such sufferings as an honor; since I do not doubt that it goes with me as it did with Ephraim, who was innocently imprisoned for the sake of a murderer, because he had once killed a cow out of foolishness.

I know well that I encounter nothing unfavorable in words or deeds that I have not otherwise earned many times over in relation to my Savior and to my neighbor. That is why I certainly lament the injury, [but] I do not complain. [Rather] in spite of that I wish that my readers would not be disturbed by my reputation, [and would] let these truths of the cross work in their hearts. I can have that ambition rightly that some [will see beyond my reputation], because I do it myself: I read the sermons of Bileam with great edification. With any presentation I do not even once examine the person, but rather the grounds. I do not even believe my most trusted friends without grounds, and I believe dutifully from the heart all truths that come from the mouth of an opponent.

So then, dear reader, may you be a little prepared for the useful application of these pages. May my dear Savior be so friendly to you all that you must feel ashamed. It happens that way to me every day, because I may not lift up my eyes toward him. He is the most gracious Lord of the entire world. I am a sinner, [and this experience] happens to me when I become inwardly aware of the nearness of his presence, but because of that I want to beg him not to go (Luke 5:8), but rather to stay (Luke 24:29).

Marienborn [Germany]

26 August 1738

IN THESE SPEECHES COUNT ZINZENDORF OFFERS REFLECTIONS ON THE main point, the heart of Christian faith, by explicating this passage from Luther's *Small Catechism*.

"I believe that Jesus Christ, who is truly God begotten of the Father from eternity and also truly human born in time of the virgin Mary, is my Lord; that he redeemed me, a lost and condemned human being; that he purchased and won me from all sin, from death, and from the dominion of the devil, not with gold or silver but with his holy precious blood and with his innocent suffering and dying so that I might belong to him, live under him in his kingdom and serve him in eternal righteousness, blamelessness, and blessedness; likewise that he rose from the dead, lives and reigns in eternity. This is most certainly true."[1]

1. Martin Luther, in Tappert, *Book of Concord*, 345.

The First Speech
(23 February 1738)

I Believe

"You believe that there is one God. You do well in that. The devils believe too, and tremble" (James 2:19). This is a clear proof that it is not enough for salvation to believe that there exists only one God. "Therefore, God so loved the world that he gave his only begotten Son, in order that all who believe in him should not be lost but rather have eternal life" (John 3:19). And the Gospel exists for this purpose, "that you may believe Jesus is the Christ, the Son of God, and that you might have life through faith in his name" (John 20:31).[1]

Our faith is distinguished from that of the devils in this way. We believe in the name of the One called "Jesus" because he will save his

---

1. In this speech Count Zinzendorf expresses his theological opposition to so-called rational or natural religion. Intellectuals in the eighteenth century found very appealing the idea that all actual, historical religions share a common core. This core was thought to consist of a simple set of religious ideas that constituted the truth of any and all religion. Thus, the actual teachings and practices of a religion were not to be taken seriously except insofar as they expressed these core ideas. Lord Herbert of Cherbury set forth the core in this way: 1) there is one supreme God; 2) this God ought to be worshipped; 3) the connection between piety and virtue is the most important part of religious practice; 4) people must repent of their wickedness and vices; and 5) there is reward or punishment after this life (cf. Cherbury's little book *De Veritate*, published in Paris in 1624). These tenets were thought to be rational because they were imagined to be discoverable within every religion by all truly rational people. They were said to be natural because they were thought to be written into the fabric of nature. There are several telling philosophical and anthropological objections to this view. But Zinzendorf found it religiously and theologically objectionable from the perspective of Christian teaching. Some of his reasons appear in this speech.

people, he will deliver his people from their sins (Matthew 1:21). One must come to know the name properly.

The Lord foresaw that people would think belief in God to be sufficient for salvation, therefore he countered: "Believe in me" (John 14:1). Whether we suppose there is a God or not is not up to us. We believe by nature. Certainly there are many who wish deep in their hearts that there were no God (Psalm 14:1), so that they could sin more freely. But deep down they cannot believe there is none. The highest peaks of reason can neither remove the idea from the depths of the self, nor hinder and dampen the recognition of the great Supreme Being. The foundation is laid too deeply in nature and in the heart. That people know there is a God is manifest in them, since God revealed it to them.[2] Since the Enemy of souls cannot now prevent people from taking notice of God (he must even do it himself), he gladly persuades them that he has saving faith. One might admit as valid that there is one God and feel fear at his name because he can punish, chastise, afflict, and damn. As a result one does not sin with such abandon anymore, and this produces worldly people who are honorable and upright. But few people know and believe anything substantial about Christ. One need not reach beyond the bounds of Christendom to see this. Many so-called Christians believe the same thing that the nations who follow Muhammad's teaching believe, the same thing that the Jews believe: in only one God. (Jews exclude Jesus. Muslims omit his true nature although they think of him with deep reverence.) These so-called Christians name the glorious name of Jesus in all manner of circumstances, and allow themselves to be named after him, only somewhat more superficially. Jesus, the great Jesus, whom all the angels of God shall worship, before whom every knee on earth shall bow and all authorities lay their crowns in the dust. To be sure the name appears on people's lips when it is the custom in

2. The Count grants the advocates of rational or natural religion this point: existence itself drives us to be religious. Every person organizes life, and must do so, according to some fundamental convictions and commitments. By means of these one unifies personality and life, makes sense of experience, and understands the self's role in the cosmos. The object of these commitments and convictions is that which concerns us ultimately, on which our being or not being depends, i.e., our god. Zinzendorf notes here in his own way that all people recognize a god, a high essence or Supreme Being, a main thing in life. But simply to have a god of some sort, even a highly moral one, is not enough to grant participation in what Christians call salvation. Even atheists can be very religious about their atheism! But one must know the true God. It is only the true and actual God who is able to save.

a country or city, since this, too, has its fashion. But it is always rare when a person whose reason, reputation, property, or talent sets them only a little above the vulgar mob mentions the Savior often. Most hold that nothing more is necessary to being an honest and upright person than to be respectful before God. But when things have sunk so low in a country or city that key people, the very people upon whom others depend, are ashamed of the Savior and of his teaching, then one can reckon that it will soon come out according to the expression of the prophet Daniel, that Christ is no more (cf. Daniel 9:26).

For a misfortune has already gained ground in Christendom: one has dealings only with God and has very little to do with Christ, as if he had never been upon the earth and did not stand on almost every page of the Bible, or as if he really had little significance and one could believe, live, and be saved without him. That is why people regard the sayings of the Savior as trivial, that is, as fitting for the inferior schools but too coarse and improper for the wise and great people. Many who concern themselves with the Savior think and speak of him in a completely cold-minded way. Others who are considered the best and most pious among Christians believe one must require more seriousness about the knowledge of God than is customary. Since he can drag one to judgment one must honor God, fear God, and stop offending him with sin, and instead love and serve him because of his countless blessings. If others freely sin during the day, these people keep away from evil out of fear and respect. But Christ with his name and merit is unknown, and I believe if people were not sometimes terrified or did not sometimes feel pain, it would be a long time before the name "Jesus" passed their lips. It is necessary for us to take this matter rightly to heart and grasp it in our deepest selves and rightly concern ourselves with Christ: who he is according to his Person, Offices, and Status, and not only experience the power of it for ourselves but confess him before everyone and neglect no opportunity to make his name known to others. And this is the chief task of all the witnesses of Jesus, who have perceived and known him, that they always paint the Savior—who is so unknown—before the eyes of the whole world, and especially before so-called Christendom. Because even if they say: "One must know him, one must have him in one's heart, one must not let him be taken from one," you can rest assured, the so-called Christian world does not know him (John 16:3).

One does not begin by first worrying about how one can leave sin behind and become pious, but rather how one can get to know Jesus as one's own Savior, since the former will follow all by itself, after the Son has once made one free; since he alone can free from sin, he alone can help and counsel in matters for which no human counsel is adequate. We cannot deny that we have sin in us (I John 1:8), and that we carry it upon ourselves until we go to our graves. For this reason the body is dead because of sin (Romans 8:10), and decomposition befalls it. The reality of sin's malignant poison is so firmly fixed in nature and in the whole mass of humanity that the healthiest thing for them is to go into their graves and be reduced to absolute worthlessness, then the Savior can make something better out of them.*

But even though we carry this body of death, among children of God sin is a banished, crucified, and condemned thing, viewed as a malefactor and prisoner, which does not have to re-appear automatically and inevitably, if only the soul is no longer treacherous, nor friendly with sin. The old self has received its judgment: it is bound to be killed and negated on the cross of Christ (Romans 6:6). "For this purpose the Son of God appeared, to destroy the works of the devil" (I John 3:8), to dissolve the structure and principle of sin and tear it asunder in order that it might not come to desire, deed, and death among believers, and instead the sinful corruption remain underfoot, its power, might, and dominion lost, [that] it might be subject, no longer allowed to be active, nor always to have to await a new execution.**

---

* [Count Zinzendorf wrote this note himself. He thought this point needed clarification.] At least human souls can already be cleansed here in time, but the remaining elements of human persons are not cleansed prior to the grave. Then, when souls that were in the body with sin leave their tents, a pure soul without sin journeys to the Savior, and when the body which sent forth the sinless soul lies there in the grave, then it is still a sinful little body and will not be designated "totally clean" until its concentrated little kernel is transfigured.

** [Zinzendorf again added this note himself to the published edition of the speeches.] In *The Smalcald Articles* it says, "The Savior does not allow sin to hold sway and win the upper hand, so that sin is committed, but rather wards it off and restrains it, so that it [sin] is not able to do whatever it will; but if [sin] does do what it wants, then the Holy Spirit and faith are not present. For as St. John says: 'Whoever is born of God does not sin and cannot sin.' And yet it is also surely the truth (as the same St. John writes) 'Therefore if we say we have no sin, we lie, and God's truth is not in us.'" Vid. Libr. Conc. Edit. Reinecc. p. 511. [[Translator's note: *The Smalcald Articles* were penned by Martin Luther as a theological testament; cf. William Russell, *Luther's Theological Testament*. Zinzendorf may be quoting from memory here because he actually misquotes Luther.

It is not even necessary for a believer to listen to sin, much less get mixed up in a fight with it, rather since the solemn divorce of the absolved and purified soul from its old husband has taken place through the corpse of Christ, [the believer] must renounce [sin]; therefore now one can serve the true Husband in peace and fruit can be brought to him unto eternal life; one is neither willing, nor inclined, nor compelled to sin anymore.[3]

This freedom is given to us as a blessedness and a privilege. But no one is to seek it prior to grace, much less is it to be placed above grace, but rather grace must be there first, and in the quality of a godless person one must have obtained the forgiveness of sins, after that follows the privilege that one is no longer compelled to sin and may be godly. One acquires forgiveness through faith in the name of the only begotten Son of God. Without this there is no life, no grace, no forgiveness. Our faith must stand fast on the merit of the Savior, who died for us that he might deliver us from all unrighteousness and purify a people for himself to be his own possession, that they might be industrious workers of good.

Luther wrote that the Holy Spirit does not permit sin to rule, whereas Zinzendorf says it is the Savior, i.e. Jesus, who does not permit it. Cf., the *Book of Concord*, 310. But of course the Spirit is the Spirit of Christ. Moreover, classical Christian teaching has it that what one Person of the holy Trinity does the other two participate in. Thus, the triune God is always fully and completely present and active even if speech refers only to one or another of the eternal "Persons".]]

---

3. This way of talking about sin and godliness belongs fully to the ancient Christian tradition. It appears in classical form in the writings of Augustine, the great bishop of Hippo in North Africa from the late fourth century to the early fifth century. He had said it like this: "When humanity by free will sinned . . . the freedom of the will was lost . . . Accordingly, the one who is the servant of sin is free to sin. And hence [one] will not be free to do right, until, being freed from sin, [one] shall begin to be the servant of righteousness. And this is true liberty . . ." *Enchiridion*, chapter 30. Thus, for Augustine, apart from the grace of God in Jesus Christ, one is free only to sin. Even the virtues of the pagans are but splendid vices because their acts do not proceed from faith in Christ (Romans 14:23) and thus can only be sin. But once having been freed by God's grace in Jesus, once having been delivered from bondage and servitude, a person is no longer compelled to sin. One is no longer bound to sin no matter what one does and has the privilege of doing righteousness in obedience to God. Augustine is quick to note that though freed from the inevitability of sin, Christians continue to sin in fact. Christians still require daily forgiveness of sins, since in this life one continues to struggle against sin and sin always remains a possibility. In this life Christians are always sinners who are nevertheless justified by grace through Jesus Christ. Luther had a great deal to say about this!

It will be necessary in all future speeches and presentations that these four questions are laid, so to speak, deep in the self.

The First: What is the sense of the word? What is meant? What is to be understood by it? Therefore, one has to say the meaning of the thing simply, bluntly and without beating around the bush, so that each person might be able to grasp and perceive the main point.

The Second: Does the meaning have a foundation: is it in agreement with Scripture? Since one must neither speak nor think of spiritual things apart from the Holy Scriptures. One knows that the truth is grounded, which brings us to the Third Question: Am I like this? Have I experienced and known this? And finally the Fourth: How do I come to be, experience, or know this?

One has to follow these rules with the teaching of Christ, too. It must be understood, tested, sought, and found.

What does it mean in the present to believe in the Lord Jesus? Godly people know and hold to be true that once about seventeen hundred years ago there was a particular man on earth, who was called "Jesus," and that it is just as certain that this person was God before [his incarnation], as it is that he became the Son of a human being afterwards; that he died for us human beings, on the cross of course, in the presence of many people, both Jews and Gentiles, that he did it partly to atone by his act for our sins and for the sins of each one, and partly that he might reconcile God, [and] partly in order to break the power and structure of sin on the cross, and negate its authority on earth, so that it might no longer be allowed to rule, but rather be trampled underfoot.

The shortest way to faith is to receive Christ (John 1:12). "To as many as received him, he gave the power to be God's children, that is, to become people who believe in his name." In his day many of his own people did not receive him. He counted for little with his lowly, poor demeanor: "We esteemed him not," says Isaiah 53. But his word and Gospel were effective among some people, so that he once had gathered together more than five hundred brothers who adored him.

We do not see the Savior in a physical way, (which does not help anyway, as we perceive with the people of his own day) therefore we also cannot receive him in a physical manner, as the disciples of his time received his physical and visible presence in the world; but the word of Christ is just as near to us, and makes the secret of the cross just as clear as if the Lord hung before our very eyes. We must believe this word and testimony about him, and both reflect on and preserve it with the very same simplicity and sincerity as the ancients, as soon as we become aware of it intensively, so that the word is spoken in the Spirit, and the power of God comes upon the heart, overcoming us like a fire and desiring to inflame us. If the Lord did not work upon souls in this actual manner, he neither could nor would blame anyone for their unbelief.

But we are still concerned with the words and actions of the Savior, and to be sure in the sight of precisely the same Spirit, through whom so many thousand people were converted at the time of the apostles. If we believe him simply and directly, then we will come to know the power of the truth that Jesus is near to our souls in a special way, that he is the Deliverer and Husband of us all. That word "believe" is an obligation, and the only law upon which salvation depends. We must trust in his primary name, "Jesus," a Redeemer, Savior, Bringer of salvation, since he must save his people from their sins (Matthew 1:21). We must believe: 1) That he is a Savior of sinners, who died for the sins of the whole world; 2) That he hung on the cross as an evildoer in the form of sinful flesh, between two murderers, and therefore was despised, rejected, wounded, and broken out of love for souls; 3) That he bought, reconciled, and saved us, and loved us so much that he gave up his life for us, so that he should have first claim on us, because he regarded our souls as so important and paid such a heavy price for them.

It is in this glorious name of the Redeemer that we must believe. To reason this is a matter too significant, solemn, and difficult, and [reason] may indeed still call faith, to which all children are directed according to their feeling and condition: "The Lord's nuisance." There are several occurrences of this designation in the old sayings of Scripture. Therefore, so many people do not want to have anything to do with [faith], and if they try it, they deal with it superficially and turn back again, because they neither can nor wish to believe. That is the only reason so many souls are lost, not because they have sinned, but rather on account of unbelief; since without faith it is impossible to please God (Hebrews 11:6).

It is true sinning must cease as well. For whoever allows sin to rule, or is compelled to let sin reign, has no faith in Christ; faith does not allow us to sin (Romans 6:2). Joyfulness in sin drives the pleasure-bound spirit. But it is likewise true, that transgressing is not the cause of rejection according to the New Testament. It is on account of unbelief that one cannot enter into rest (Hebrews 4:6). Therefore, faith is a special blessing of grace and gift of God, so that whoever has it in simplicity and naiveté can neither think of nor worship God enough.

One point, which is so difficult to many that they prefer to do and suffer all things; one cause of so many religious exercises, which are many thousand times more difficult than faith, but which are all devised only in order that they might take the place of faith. Accordingly, the art of faith is a narrow way and narrow gate which so few find (Matthew 7:14), because in point of fact it depends on nothing except that we want to let ourselves be helped; since the whole plea in Christ's stead consists only in that we should allow ourselves to be reconciled (2 Corinthians 5:20). Thereafter, free grace makes, gives, and does all the rest. (A secret hidden from most people!) They do not understand it, because they are either too superficial or too melancholy, and prefer to let themselves be morose and bitter. God wills to bestow grace upon all sinners on account of Christ, and by grace to cast natural sin and natural religion into a heap.

The genuine sinner has the first, greatest, and more direct claim and comes nearer and more easily to grace. When a scoundrel is converted it is a plain miracle; but when a pious person is saved, it is a double marvel and an extraordinary success. Scripture says Christ died thus for the godless (Romans 5:6); and he himself speaks along the same line when he says he did not come to call the righteous (Luke 5:32). By nature we are all equally sinners and equally godless before God; but this situation is so concealed and so hidden by means of reason and education that people often no longer know themselves. One person condemns another wholeheartedly for being a sinner, and ignores the fact that he condemns himself along with the other. "You are the man of death," said Nathan to David, who had thought to condemn another. Many a person has had neither opportunity nor provocation to sin, and therefore could not become aware of the true condition of the heart; should such a one have time, occasion, training, and capacity, they probably will sin more crudely and abusively than all others; since sin is truly planted in the heart of one and all, only more disguised, more hidden, more deceptive and more dangerous [in those who believe themselves to be without sin]. Indeed, such people express greater enmity toward the Savior, greater unbelief, and greater fury over the propriety of grace.

Generally speaking it is a bad method to pass judgment on people solely because of what they do; but it is even worse to conclude from the omission of one act or another that nothing of the evil inclination is left.[4] "The Lord looks upon the heart" (1 Samuel 16:7). Deeds belong in the worldly court of law, and must be judged and punished there, which is nothing either more or less than fair. But the divine jurisdiction goes deeper, to the very heart and motive, in judging good and evil things.[5]

Therefore, we must come to Jesus as sinners, and declare ourselves, according to our hearts and minds, to be godless, fornicating, drunken, insolent, ferocious or lying people, and that disposition and mind will be changed, [we must] seek the grace and blood-won justification of the One who makes the godless righteous. The most innocent, the most pious, the person who has probably been so blameless from the moment of emerging from the womb to the present that one would have to take him for an angel on account of his good training, in relation to whom one neither hears nor sees anything evil, this very person [bears] the same appraisal and damnation as the most immoral sort of human beings among [us]. None is better on account of his little tidbit of good, and none is more wicked because of his many evil acts. All need grace, mercy, and a Savior's blood; before God none [of our works] carry any weight, neither our scampering and running about, nor our repentance and improvement, but rather his mercy alone, Christ's atonement, satisfaction, and reconciling offering on the cross. To be sure, one can abuse this precious truth in the direction of safety and irresponsibility; but nevertheless it is and remains the truth pure and simple. This even pro-

---

4. It is very interesting that Zinzendorf should use the phrase "evil inclination" here. It has a long history in the Jewish tradition. Since ancient times rabbis have spoken of two inclinations in each person. The *yetzer ha-tov*, the good inclination, and the *yetzer ha-rah*, the bad inclination, are said to strive for mastery of the heart of every person. Paul seems to have been thinking in this tradition in Romans 7. One wonders where Zinzendorf picked up this way of talking. It may have been from rabbis and Jews he knew, or it might simply have come from his reflection on Paul's writings in the New Testament.

5. Zinzendorf's point turns on the distinction between mere civil righteousness and righteousness before God. One could be blameless before the worldly court of law, but at the same time be utterly damned as wicked before God. Since God looks upon the heart and motive, true obedience means doing God's will with a pure and joyful heart with no regard for consequences or rewards. It means loving and obeying God with abandon and purely for God's own sake. One's civil righteousness has only an ambiguous and uncertain relationship to that!

duces unity in religion, but is, as far as that goes, almost the only true and proper controversy about reality. This also makes the leading and tending of souls concise and easy. If each one understands himself to be a sinner in his own way, and humbles himself before grace, then befalls him what is meant for the eminent and well deserving.

There are so many different kinds of people, and Satan has bound them by means of so many different kinds and modes of evil, or deceived them with various appearances of good, that one could certainly not disentangle them from each other, if there were not also a universal sickness for which a medicine was suitable. But thus one can now say to souls, that all human beings require grace, the respectable just as much as the profligate, so that all need Christ's blood, which alone cancels the future wrath, conquers Satan and hell, cleanses the heart, cures injuries, pulls the love of sin out by the roots, and can produce all good.

We are sinners in our best works and actions as well as with our greatest acts of sin. No intention, no matter how good, helps without Christ, either to free from sin, or to be godly and do good. Consequently, one must really concern oneself only about faith in Christ, but let all other things quickly go; and forget about them like a child. And Jesus must become our faith, our love, and our hope, the only object and purpose of our life: all thinking, speaking, and desiring must become completely his; then they are right and fitting before God because of Christ.

In faith we need not tremble like the devils, but instead can be sincere and confident like children.

The Second Speech
(26 February 1738)

Jesus!

AND THERE IS NO OTHER NAME GIVEN TO HUMAN BEINGS, BY WHICH we can be saved (Acts 4:12). It is our fortress and our free city to which we must flee for deliverance (Proverbs 18:10; Numbers 35:15, 28). Very few people understand this. The angel of God told Mary what it meant: "You shall call his name Jesus; because he will save (deliver) his people from their sins" (Matthew 1:21).

The explanation and exposition of this name was necessary for two reasons, first because the Jews hoped out of their particular feelings for the Messiah as king, and saw [the matter] only from [the perspective of] their external affliction, burden, and trouble, as people are generally so created by nature that they know of no other torment than bodily burdens and public nuisances, and are difficult to convince that sin is the greatest affliction, so that the prophet marvels: "What do the people complain about? Each one grumbles against his sins" (Lamentations 3:39). Secondly, [the explanation] was necessary because otherwise they could have made the deduction from old examples of divine rescue, [that] their Shiloh was even one of the ancient helpers, whom God so often sent to them when they were in trouble and whom they asked him to send: those [helpers] were the Judges, who delivered the people from their enemies, and renewed the lost rule of God time and again among the people; therefore they were also called the saviors of the people.

The Jews might easily have thought of the name in terms of the yoke of the Romans. Therefore, the old prophets said, "Your king comes to you meekly" (Zechariah 9:9). With that the idea of Gideon and

Samson and Jephthah and Barak is cancelled. Consequently, John was sent to make clear to the people that the promised salvation consisted in something different, namely in the forgiveness of sins (Luke 1:77). And on the basis of this first principle the angel, too, testified that the Savior will deliver his people from the misery, rule and power of sin. "He appeared that he might take away our sins" (l John 3:5).

But who are the people he will deliver? Here the Jews will be properly understood, to whom he chiefly professed his loyalty. "I am not sent, except to the lost sheep of the house of Israel" (Matthew 15:24). "He came to his own, to his own people" (John 1:11). But his office nowhere carried less weight than in his fatherland and among his own people, and the Jews did not accept him as their Messiah; because they wanted to have a physical king of Israel, who would be no lackey of the Roman Overseers, like the four princes[1] who had to carry on with cunning and politics, but rather [a king] who would make the people prosperous through a declared earthly kingdom; thus the Gentiles were chosen for the spiritual kingdom, yes the whole world, and now the word "his people" has a great and wide extent. "I have still other sheep," says our Savior, "Who are not of this fold, who I must bring here" (John 10:16).

We are not of the Jewish line and fold, but rather by grace came to it, and shall in a certain degree fill that position. Therefore, Matthew 28:19 says, "Go out into all the world, and preach the Gospel to all creatures, beginning in Jerusalem"; and Acts 1:8 says, "You shall preach in Jerusalem, and in the whole of Judea and Samaria, and to the ends of the earth." That was the Savior's wish and desire, because he had come to cast a fire upon the earth that it might soon be kindled. He is a Savior for all people (1 Timothy 4:10). But his believers experience, enjoy, and make use of it. The apostles extol salvation in all their speeches and writings, so that everyone who wants to have it might possess an interest in it and hope for it. Since Jesus is the universal Restorer of the whole human community, and a propitiation not only for our sins, but rather for the sins of the whole world (1 John 2:2). The old fence and dividing wall is struck down, the gulf is filled in, in order that even those who are far away might become nearer through the blood of Christ (Ephesians 2:14, 17).

---

1. The tetrarchs, each of whom ruled a region of the Roman Near East under close Roman watch.

This is not opposed to the sayings of John 17:2 and Hebrews 7:25, that he does not intercede for the whole world, but rather for his faithful ones. Because that was a Will and Testament, in which he appoints heirs and makes a bequest to be carried out. But soon after on the cross he thought not only of his own who were in the world, whom he loved to the end, but rather he also thought of the crucifiers, of his enemies, of the greatest sinners, of evildoers, and prayed for them all (Isaiah 53:12). The first demonstration of the answer [to his prayer] appeared in his nearest neighbor, who converted on account of Jesus' intercession and became his friend.

But what is the sin from which he will deliver us? Everyone knows and feels that sin is something neither good nor happy for humanity. Thus, one does not first need its description in terms of the Law; but on the authority of the Gospel one can show it in summary, from John 16. Sin is not to trust in Jesus, when one either directly hates the Savior (John 15:18, 19), or on account of one's fleshly mind has neither heart nor desire for him and his community (Romans 8:7). This enmity of unbelief goes so far that children and servants of God in whom one notices nothing otherwise offensive, indeed [in whom] great kindness is noticed, are hated only because they stand surely with him: "We cannot tolerate him before our eyes, he prides himself on being God's child" (Wisdom of Solomon 2:12–16).[2] "You must be hated by everyone on account of my name" (Matthew 10:22). *Autos ephra.*[3]

Not only in the time of the pagans was it said, "A good man; but bad because a Christian."[4] That is to say, he would be an upright man, if only he weren't a so-called Christian. But this sentiment is held in the

2. It is quite interesting that Count Zinzendorf quotes a book of the Old Testament Apocrypha. But it is unclear what it means. Did he make this reference only to add rhetorical flair? After all, it was the age of the baroque style. Or did this text simply reinforce the point he wanted to make? Furthermore, did he have a high regard for the apocryphal books? In any case, it is clear that he was familiar enough with them to quote from memory.

3. I have transliterated the Greek phrase Zinzendorf uses here. It is not a phrase that appears in this form in the New Testament. Instead, it is a Pythagorean phrase. Its import is to emphasize a subject already known. A Koine construction with the same meaning does appear several times in the New Testament. One example is Mark 8:29: "And he [himself] said to them, 'But who do you say that I am?'" The opening phrase in this verse places the emphasis on the subject, Jesus. Zinzendorf likewise emphasizes the subject, Jesus again, for whose sake one must endure hatred.

4. Zinzendorf quotes this saying in Latin.

very midst of Christendom. As is generally known , it is no particular merit or quality for a follower of Jesus to stick to the book. How little honor is gotten with the message of Jesus? How much insult and pressure on the other hand are bound up with it?

To be sure, not many people pay attention to the witnesses of Jesus, because to these witnesses love for Christ's cross and bliss with their Lord is more dear to them than anything; they know that he himself was treated no better, that he was persecuted first and most of all (John 15:18), and that their humiliation is nothing compared to the contempt which he had to experience in his life ("We took no notice of him," says Isaiah in the name of the Jews, "He was the most despised and least esteemed"; see 53:3), compared to the affront which he still daily has to suffer from the world. And if Paul says in 2 Corinthians 12:15, "I love much, and am loved little"; it is multiplied in the case of our Lord, who in suffering as in all things has pre-eminence.

Just consider the wretched idea, attention and opinion which we ourselves had of him and in relation to him from childhood on; what a poor submission of the heart, what thanklessness in relation to his merit, what estrangement from following him, what a secret fear in the presence of his people because we were all called Christians and were baptized in his name. Thus sin lies in unbelief and expresses itself in an indifference, alienation, deviation, and cold-mindedness toward the Lord, or in open enmity with and rebellion against him. The outbreak of the deed (for which conscience and law punishes) is only the fruit and testimony of the inner corruption and wicked motives of the heart, in which sin is actually to be sought, and according to which people are of two sorts: first, completely dead; second, awakened to life.

Those who with their corruption are completely dead and insensible, that is, cool-headed and composed, come to be thought of in part as fine, honorable, quiet, yes, even pious and God-fearing people, as if they still had a feeling of God and conscience, a sense of the numinous.[5] But they are without feeling for the Savior and are indifferent and cold-minded toward the true good; with respect to the Savior they are without him, that is to say, without God. Moreover, they can often to be sure intend good, they can look closely at much good in the understanding and in the depths of the self through presentations of the divine Word and the power of prevenient grace, or they can also be excited at times

---

5. Zinzendorf employs the Latin phrase *Sensum Numinis*.

by solid inferences and thoughts, but it goes no further than fantasy, or reason, then vanishes again and cannot be from God because it does not remain. (If its source were God the person would abide in him. 1 John 3:6, 9). It surely happens that those people are not hostile and obstructive to the rule of Christ, yes they are even useful to and promotive of it, and they love the good; but their hearts remain stone.

They can also grasp that they are good for nothing and are in poverty, but it is only a fleeting thought; at the same time they remain lazy, negligent, and carefree and cannot get a handle on their very selves. They have no power to help themselves, but rather remain lying in death. Still, they remain well-disposed toward the good, and their hearts are a tender object of the Savior, so that when he sees his time and they are brought to the sign of grace, they soon can be helped; it might be that they are too well pleased in their present circumstances and through them perish wretchedly.

Such dead people are either virtuous, finally able to go so far in the false piety and improvement allowed by Satan that they progress in spirituality to the angels; or they are corrupt. Even though they live in all sins just the same, these people do not blaspheme, but rather allow the good to stand, like Felix: because they are dead to spiritual things; and there is with those same people, if they are not met at a sensitive corner, almost the same circumstance [as Felix], (and then it amounts to a manner of life).

Others in the category of unbelief are not dead, but rather living and active enough, enlivened and invigorated by the spirit of the world and stirred up by hell (James 3:6). They bear the image of the devil and are declared, public, trained, yes truly purchased enemies of the rule of Christ. They diligently seek to hinder by all sorts of ways and methods, and make it a special merit and religious duty to let themselves be instruments against the work and the servants of God; they often have no glory and benefit, but rather detriment and shame because of it and they do it anyway. Such people are truly dangerous sinners and tools of Satan and indeed they even become his martyrs: they are almost unconquerable; and because they are hard, yes almost impossible, to persuade on account of the deeply established foundation of their sin, the Lord must employ highly unusual means for their salvation if it is ever to come about at all.

They are, to repeat, either virtuous like Saul, who even greatly raged and believed that he had to do many terrible things against the name of Jesus, while at the same time he was blameless and pious according to the Law; or they are corrupt and vicious, who in their crude wrongdoing have occasionally become mockers and enemies of the truth. Those women and men who serve Christ are intolerable to look upon because they rebuke and censure such evil-doing, as the matter finds expression in the Book of Wisdom,[6] and Herod is a biblical example of it (Mark 6: 18–19). All these sorts are wretched and lost and need a Savior who could help them out of this predicament, if they are willing and obliged to be saved.

But what does salvation mean? It means one is torn from the ruling authority of darkness and one is placed within the ruling authority of Jesus. He will help the dead out of their death, bring the slaves of Satan to freedom, take away enmity and unbelief, and give faith and love in their place.

The Lord himself must make a beginning for such a salvation: since no saying of Jesus about people demands that they should begin and help themselves, rather the Savior said, "I will draw them all to me. They only have to let themselves be saved and reconciled." He will do it all through his Spirit. Cast fire upon the earth and pour out his love upon all hearts, yes even breathe the breath of life into the dead. One must only be still and wait and be attentive to the voice of the Lord when he comes to the heart with his power, his fire, his promptings, and his Spirit, and thereafter not talk things over with flesh and blood but be obedient to the heavenly visitation.

God sees according to his wisdom, so he can make an impression on each soul in the best, that is, most effective, way. The methods, occasions, and hours are different for all so that one cannot determine it. The Lord takes hold of one in preaching, another in his house, overcomes a third in the street, another again out in the field, and seizes a fifth in the very act of sinning. Therefore, it is not in accordance with the Gospel to lay down fixed rules, or to set forth methods[7] and forms in which souls

6. Zinzendorf makes another reference to the same apocryphal book quoted earlier.

7. Zinzendorf uses the Latin *methodismum* and rejects any sort of mold, or one-size-fits-all process, for effecting conversion. He denies there is any one way the Lord reaches people and denies that there can be any one way to preach or to engage in ministry with people. One must be sensitive to the Lord's leading and work and go with it. One must let one's own program go.

must first be situated, or to expect a coincident method in the seeking and gathering of souls. One must entrust to the Savior's free grace and judgment how he can and will reach souls.

But in the meantime he is indeed willing and ready to receive all souls with prevenient grace.[8] Therefore it is inexcusable, an atrocious sin, if one seeks to elude and avoid the Holy Spirit when he[9] comes to the soul with divine power, or is frivolous, light-minded and neglectful of the Spirit's drawing near. Then one can often miss a moment upon which great grace and salvation depended, a moment which one cannot bring back again for days or years, and which one seeks fruitlessly for a long time, until the Holy Spirit, who in the meantime returned to his place again (Hosea 5:15), returns in grace.[10] Therefore, one must leave everything lie just as it is when such times and promptings of grace come, because all things (including the most important commercial dealings in the world) can be retrieved except this visitation itself. Indeed, if someone were in church and felt the Holy Spirit begin to preach in his heart, he should follow Dr. Luther's counsel; let the preacher one can see preach on, and attend instead to the gracious movement, in the heart, of the preacher one cannot see.

It is good to notice this, in order that one not make a mess of, hinder, and stop the work of God, but rather make it firm and durable

8. The Lutheran Formula of Concord, which I suspect Zinzendorf has in mind here, teaches that the proclamation of repentance and the promise of the Gospel extends to all people (Tappert, *The Book of Concord*, 619–20).

9. Whenever Zinzendorf uses a personal pronoun, he uses the one that is grammatically correct in German. In this case he uses "he" because *Geist* is a masculine noun. But he should not be taken to imply that the Holy Spirit is actually masculine, any more than one should think that the terms "Father" and "Son" applied to God have any actual gender reference. Cf., Kinkel, *Our Dear Mother the Spirit*.

10. Zinzendorf appropriates and repeats here the view of his teacher, August Hermann Francke. The claim is that there are certain moments or times of grace. These are times when God "draws near" and overcomes a person, drawing one into faith, or more deeply into faith or more faithful life. There can be no preparation for these times, since we are totally dependant on God's grace. One cannot produce these times by means of any human skill or power. God simply creates them. The Formula of Concord states this total dependence upon God's grace like this: "2. We also reject the error of the crass Pelagians, who taught by his own powers, without the grace of the Holy Spirit, man can convert himself to God, believe the Gospel, wholeheartedly obey God's law, and thus merit forgiveness of sins and eternal life. 3. We also reject the error of the Semi Pelagians, who teach that man by virtue of his own powers could make a beginning of his conversion but could not complete it without the grace of the Holy Spirit" (Tappert, *Book of Concord*. 471).

with prayer and supplication. It can even happen in a person's heart this briefly, when one has no other opportunity, "Lord! Have mercy! Lord, be gracious to me, a sinner!" This carries just as much weight with God, as if one had spoken many words; since Moses himself spoke no words at all (Exodus 14:15), that is to say, he just cried out. But at the same time it must be nothing compulsory and feigned, but rather free and brought about by the grace of God, because otherwise one impedes both self and others. One must simply allow grace to have a free run in all its work, until faith has been joined with the Word (see Hebrews 4:2 as a foundation text). This does not come about because of deep understanding, great aptitude, courage and worthiness, or even from a journey of soaring genius beyond the divine boundary, but rather from the free mercy of God in the order of grace.

The cause of all grace is to be sought in the merits and sufficiency of Christ alone. He must become and remain the only source of our salvation, and must matter and have value for us; he must be effective for us, only in his bloody form on the cross. Because on the cross he himself was baptized with a baptism of blood, and consecrated as the Savior of the world, his name, "Jesus," was sealed for us unto all eternity. Therefore, whoever understands the mystery of the cross and the wounds of Jesus can have comfort and counsel, even if he were the greatest sinner, because Jesus atoned for all sins that have taken place and all that will take place unto eternity. He confessed for the whole world when he said from the cross, "Father, forgive them'" And when he called out, "It is accomplished"; he pronounced at the same time a general absolution over the whole world. Thus, whoever now believes in him will not be judged (John 3:18).

In addition one need not worry now that souls do not humble themselves enough and become contrite on account of their sins. All have to experience a true form of abasement by grace; it is necessary for as many as the Savior perceives [living] under other motives, with every single one, to break his mind and to transform and convert him; "Indeed, the taste of the powerful reconciliation itself must serve to [evoke] true abasement."[11] For as on the Day of the Lord those who are found still living, to whom it is not prevented, are thus raised up out of

---

11. This is a hymn text and rhymes in German. Using Zinzendorf's spelling it is as follows: "Ja selbst das schmekken vom kraeftgen Versuehnen, das muss zu wahrer demuethigung dienen."

their decomposition [before they experience anything else] (what the others who were dead experienced slowly and without feeling, the living must undergo in an instant and probably more uncomfortably, as regards the transformation of their mortality into immortality and their corruption into incorruption) in the same way some are able to experience in an instant or in a few hours everything that others feel over the course of days and years; because the circumstances with such guidance of souls appear incomprehensible and the obstacles seem in some cases insurmountable. Therefore one can dictate nothing to the Savior concerning [the] mortification and pardoning of wretched sinners, but rather one must entrust it all to him and his wisdom and faithfulness alone, how many he thinks it proper to allow to experience, each one, the dread, and how soon he can with this and that be ready to persuade and save [the sinner]. To be sure, his desire is to deliver and help soon. "Your king comes to you, a Deliverer and a Helper" (Zechariah 9:9).

The Savior's method is not to command that souls go through a long process of penitence and preparation, but rather only a true and heartfelt word is required; thus grace is present and has helped one out of all sins. And actually the greatest wretchedness is when one has not the Savior and has not love; as on the other hand that is heaven on earth to live in the grace and love of the Savior: thus it is a great benefit that no one is more eager than he to disclose himself to the soul as Savior, so that no one would rather give faith; for he surely bears salvation to us.

If we now usually gladly think about things which can contribute something to our advantage and use; so it is easy in stillness also to think about this matter by which we once can say out of our own experience: He can save forevermore; "He can deliver all who come to him." Then, after that: I will recount all that he has done in my soul (Psalm 66:16).

The Third Speech
(2 March 1738)

Christ

WE HAVE FOUND THE MESSIAH, IN GREEK "*CHRIST*," IN GERMAN, "*DEN Gesalbten*" [the Anointed] (John 1:41). The name was already given to him often in the Old Testament and for those believers was an oil poured out on and on (Song of Solomon 1:3).

He must first prove himself to souls in all respects as Jesus [in his humanity], after that they also feel that he is the Christ. After the announcement of grace through his blood one also partakes of the oil of his priesthood (Psalm 133:2), the anointing (1 John 2:27).

The name "Jesus" is his proper name as a human being, which he bears just as he bears our flesh and blood; and it is for all, let them be as dead or as sick, as wretched, poor, and sinful, as they can be, they are able and shall acquire life and salvation through his name. But the name "Christ" is a special name for his office and is appropriate only for those who are already saved and are his again.[1] Because they will be anointed by him, their great High Priest, as priests of God. That name has to do with the general intercession for sinners on the cross: "Father, forgive them"; but this refers to the last testament of Jesus, which he made with his Father when he prayed only for those whom the Father had given him (John 17:9), and not for the whole world.

---

1. Zinzendorf's remark here is based on the fact that the German word for "Christian" is *Christ*. Therefore, Master and disciple share the same title. But the Count holds the view that this title is appropriate only for those people who sincerely and authentically belong to Jesus Christ from the heart; who cling to him in life and death; who are willing and happy to lose everything for his sake.

The name is also essential and venerable, because the Father himself affixed his seal to it and consecrated it for him (John 6:27; 10:36). The Father appointed Jesus both Lord and Christ (Acts 2:36). "Do not provoke him," it said in the Old Covenant: "My Name is in him" (Exodus 23:21). One has to grieve so much the more then, when the name "Christ" is regarded so wretchedly and abused: and there are those who carried it so far, and have so little consideration for his rank, that in his presence they are deeply ashamed and tremble over their foolhardiness.

We call all people [in all denominations] Christians and truly so, the name does not belong to us only; one should name "so-called Christians"[2] people who support the religion and doctrine of Christ, declare their allegiance to him externally and announce they are for him; and I wish this name [so-called Christian] were not only more established than the religious title which we use daily, but had already been in common use for a long time.[3] Thus the Gentiles named the first witnesses after the foundation of their religion.

But the name "Christ" belongs jointly to the Head and to his true members. It even won some people over to his side, in which sense Luther reportedly once said, "I am a Christ." It is clear that at one time such people fought back and forth, with cause and truth, over the fact that Christ was named daily in everyone's ears. Whoever wants truly to be called "Christian" [German: *Christ*] must be able to say truthfully: "I live, yet not I, but Christ lives in me" (Galatians 2:20). After all, it is certain that the community is called "Christ" in the Scriptures. "For just as the body is one and has many members, and all members of the body, though many, are one body, so it is with Christ" (1 Corinthians 12:12).

2. Zinzendorf uses the term *Christianer* here to name people who are Christian in name only, in outward and casual observance, but without inward passion and devotion.

3. The point, of course, is that Zinzendorf longs for a publicly recognized distinction between those who confess Jesus Christ with mouth alone, but who lack passion for the Savior and his cross, who do not want Jesus to interfere with their lives, intentions, and goals, and those for whom Jesus Christ is the love of their hearts, who hang on his every word and deed, and who desire above all to become like him. Zinzendorf wanted people both inside and outside the Christian Church to see the difference between people who use the Savior for their own purposes, or who remain detached or casual about him, and people who long to be used by Jesus for his purposes, for whom Jesus is life, hope, love, and all things. *Christianer* names those external confessors, and the German word *Christ* names those who desire Jesus and surrender themselves to him.

And it is reasonable. One should call her "woman," since she was taken from man (Genesis 2:23).[4]

Now the name is so great that one cannot worthily speak of it, and it might well be commanded: "Let it be just as if a person were silent and let all mortal remains tremble at the suspicion of his presence." I am not powerful enough to describe a name that comprises in itself so many mysteries, blessings, functions, and happinesses.[5] To be sure, a soul which accordingly comes to know him truly must still more lie in the dust before the throne of his Lordship and be dragged there, so to speak, from the breast of Jesus before the feet of the Messiah, on account of humility, shame, and a deeper understanding of its own unworthiness.[6]

Since Christ is called the anointed according to excellence. He has all those things alone and in himself, in the highest degree and excellence, that they who were called anointed in the Old Testament had together. There were three holy persons who were anointed. First, the

4. Zinzendorf's reference to Genesis likens the relationship between the terms *woman* and *man* to that between the application, in German, of the word *Christ* to Jesus on the one hand, and to Christians on the other. His point is that the intimacy and unity that appears in this use of the term reflects the actual intimacy and unity that exists between the Savior and his people, his disciples. The Count liked to say that the believer and the Savior say to one another, "Truly, you are bone of my bone and flesh of my flesh." The incarnation and the Gospel message itself are the twin warrants for such expressions. Moreover, Zinzendorf thought about this matter in terms of the Lutheran doctrine of the *communicatio idiomatum*—the idea that all the predicates of Jesus Christ's divinity belong fully to his humanity as well, and vice versa. Thus, Jesus in his full humanity is eternally, truly, and fully omnipresent, etc.

5. The Count speaks against the grain of modernity. Thinkers in those heady days of early modernism turned resolutely away from categories like mystery to embrace the quest for clear and distinct ideas. They forgot, or perhaps never knew, Thomas Aquinas' idea of analogical predication with respect to God. They abandoned or, again, perhaps never knew or understood, Luther's theology of the cross. They apparently found unappealing, or never considered, John Calvin's resolute refusal to regard human language as literally descriptive of God. Calvin's tendency was to regard language about God as ostensive and persuasive, not descriptive. For a helpful discussion of all this, see Placher, *The Domestication of Transcendence*. Zinzendorf further pointed to the incapacity of finite, mortal human beings to speak adequately of the glory of the name of Christ. What can be said can be said truthfully. But to specify any more than this is to reach too high for human beings.

6. Central here is Zinzendorf's conviction that we only become aware of the deep truth about ourselves in and through Jesus Christ. It is only in and through him that we learn to understand and know ourselves as sinners. It is only in and through him that we see the true seriousness, depth, and intransigence of our opposition to and rebellion against God and God's ways.

kings; second, the priests; and third, the seers or prophets of God. Our Christ bears these three names and functions, because he is called: First, the king whom God acknowledges (Psalm 2:6), and the king of all kings, the sovereign of rulers, who also creates the kings (Revelation 1:5, 19:16; and Daniel 2:21). Second, the priest after the order of Melchizedek, the high priest, like Aaron. He makes all priests of God (Revelation 1:6). Third, the great prophet mighty in deeds and words (Luke 24:19), the teacher come from God, the arch-elder of all elders who indeed directs, and who labors in words and teachings, who is the first blood-witness of the New Covenant. (They could say nothing, if Christ were not at work in them, Romans 15:18.)

I. He is himself the king of the whole world: he has universal authority, all things are directed by his breath, even the animals in the fields (Isaiah 63:14). He sustains all things through his powerful word (Hebrews 1:3). Humanity lives, moves, and has its being in him (Acts 17:28). All things must also serve him, and all this by virtue of origin, the very same original majesty and sovereignty that he had with the Father before the world was (John 17:5). But his anointing by the Father in this world is [to possess] no worldly throne, but rather human hearts. Therefore, our king of peace employs no force in his kingdom of the cross, for this reason he can also make all things subject to him (Philippians 3:21).

He suffers in his children, if it comes to the point that they must suffer. Then it often seems as if the godless people and Satan, their prince, could do whatever they want; while Christ appears to be done for, and his people to be prostrate on the ground. Because [Jesus] does not always hinder the suffering of his children; he himself suffered, and his kingdom in time is and remains a kingdom of the cross. Therefore, it is not the way of Christians to use various methods, or wealth, reputation, and power to avoid and turn away from suffering themselves. The servant is not greater than his master (John 15:20).

The Lord does not really require his power, and exercises his dominion in a hidden, mysterious way; thus his disciples as well must learn to live under oppressiveness and burdens for the sake of his honor and teaching, if they are likewise princes and lords of the world. But at those times when the Lord wants to carry something out through his servants, and it depends on neither patience nor faith, but the power of the Lord; then nothing can withstand them, they must be successful in all things, and all creatures, even their enemies themselves, must further and promote their work in the Lord. The Lordship of our king is wise and wonderful, to be worshipped in its depths. In the end, all things must bend before him and lie down at his feet; because he remains ultimately the king and judge of the whole world, and every knee, whether in heaven, on earth, or under the earth, must bow before him at his hour.

II. According to his high-priestly name he is also majestic to us. Since he is established and appointed the universal Mediator, the Deliverer and One who intercedes for us. He reconciles and purifies everything through blood. He is a true high priest to make propitiation for the sins of the people (Hebrews 2:17), and with a sacrifice he has for all time perfected all those who have been consecrated (Hebrews 10:4).

He asks on our behalf (Hebrews 7:5). "He apprises his Father of us, namely that he has done enough for us,"[7] taken the consequences and spoken well. And when the Holy Spirit brings our prayers before God through his intercession he makes them effective: and when the third article [of the creed] says that the Holy Spirit daily and abundantly forgives us our sins,[8] then we know that our sins are forgiven us indeed, in [Jesus'] name (1 John 2:12). If we also have grace immediately; then we need his blood and intercession daily, because our very best actions are so full of deficiencies and imperfections that they are worth nothing at all apart from him. We need [Jesus'] intercession eternally and we need God to be gracious to us for Jesus' sake because we have in ourselves nothing worthy or eternal. His blood speaks more emphatically and blessedly than Abel's blood, since the latter calls for vengeance over his brother; but the blood of Christ calls for grace for those who spilled it in the first place, and for us, who truly helped to shed [Jesus'] blood, because we all by nature are his enemies and his crucifiers, since we sinned in Adam, because we certainly would have sinned if it were still to be done today.[9]

---

7. A hymn text.

8. The Creed itself does not say this explicitly. Zinzendorf is referring with approval to what Luther taught that the third article of the Creed means. In Zinzendorf's mind, the Creed itself and what Luther says said about it seem to have become one and the same.

9. Count Zinzendorf's handling of the doctrine of original sin is very interesting. For centuries, under the influence of Augustine's theory, it had been understood as an inherited property. One was thought to be guilty before God because of what someone

I at least, I and my sins, "which have produced such wretchedness for you, which struck you down, and brought about your agony, which God honors!"[10] At all events we have esteemed his blood so cold-mindedly and have become as hard and insensitive to it as stones. Therefore, we have reason to bow down and to look upon his grace as a majestic grace that must be sought with a passionate desire. Now we are able to acquire grace neither with our acting nor with our penitence; neither by our promises nor our self-improvement. Therefore we should ask for grace with tears on account of God's mercy, with constant and humble submission, abandoning everything in which we once sought righteousness and salvation apart from him. We must honor the grace and sacrifice of Christ and cast ourselves down before his throne of grace as poor, miserable sinners who could not help themselves, indeed who did not even know of any help; thus shall the scepter be passed to us.

III. He is also the great teacher come from God, who makes all others into servants of God and into true prophets. He places the word of truth in their mouths. He is, amen, the true witness, the firstborn of the witnesses of the truth itself. In the past he spoke so forcefully that hearts burned within, and he must still daily pour out his Spirit and work along with the word. He compels no one to come to his Gospel, but rather the winsomeness of grace urges souls and their own wretchedness compels them that they must come to him. He is a preacher to the poor.

Simple, plain people and laity were always the most apt and the most common instruments for him, and whoever hears him must lay their own wisdom aside and become children. But what he is he also imparts to his children and makes them kingly, priestly, and prophetic people.[11] They have the honor to bear his ointment and seal and name;

---

else did. But, though this idea is still somewhat present, Zinzendorf moves in a different direction. He suggests here that sin can be thought of as our disposition to do just what Adam did. Our posture before God is like that of Adam such that if Adam's act of disobedience were still to be done, we would gladly do it. We are thus the enemies of God not because of an act external to us, the guilt for which we inherit, but rather because of the orientation of our own existence; because we ourselves want to worship and serve as God what is not the true God. Actual sins are only the expression of this fundamental orientation of the self. Moreover, by virtue of this orientation, and by virtue of our actual sins, we are in deed and truth the crucifiers of Jesus Christ.

10. Another line from a hymn.

11. This is Luther's doctrine of the "happy exchange." See Luther's powerful statement of it as the third incomparable benefit of faith in his *Von der Freiheit eines Christenmenschen*.

therefore their office is to glorify and make known the prophet par excellence, who is their master. What the husband is the wife is, too. The community is composed of nothing but princes [and princesses], who, to be sure, are hidden to the external senses, but whose deeds are a steady reflection of their Lord and Head through the whole world.

They are subject to all human order for the sake of the Lord; but their spirits have soared in freedom above every form of servanthood, which freedom the Son helps accomplish. It does not matter whether they are by nature of the caste of servants or of the free. They are even lords of their inner life (Proverbs 16:32).

The person without Christ is a slave of his pride, his apprehension and anxiety, his desire, his covetousness, of his laziness, and cannot resist but must let herself be dragged in chains from one harmful thing to another. But in Christ one overpowers, one is lord over one's cravings, is no more compelled to sin, and if one would rather not one does not have to sin.

A member of Christ's body sees sanctification or righteousness of life as a great privilege, a blessing. Faith is the Christian's obligation; to be holy is the Christian's nature. And if other people quarrel and battle round and round with sin and carnal desires, and are laid out on the ground by them after the manner of Paul's very full account in Romans 7; a member of Christ's body is positively assured that because death no more lies in store as the wages of his or her sin ("All is yours, whether life or death," 1 Corinthians 3:22), since [the Christian] has gone out of the law 's net which held him [or her] captive (but the law is the power of sin); thus also the sinful way of life must be hidden in the Christian's flesh , laid to rest by a word of God, and not be allowed to rise up again and play its part until and unless it pleases us.

Christians are priests of God who daily move along in holy adornment and lift up holy hands without wrath and doubt; they seek to become composed and manly,[12] and to remain untainted and uncon-

---

12. Interestingly, the Pietist movement was enamored of Stoic philosophy. Although Zinzendorf had shed much of the Pietism in which he had been nurtured, and even denied in print that he was a Pietist (indeed, he engaged in sharp polemics against some Pietist practices and against their general bearing), there nevertheless appears here a bit of Pietist Stoicism. The Count does not seem to notice that there is a rather acute tension between this sense of composure and "manliness" on the one hand, and the passionate devotion and loyalty to Jesus, the love for Jesus, to which he more characteristically called his hearers and readers.

taminated in all things, and they purify themselves with Christ's blood because they bear the Lord's instruments. But as priests they primarily devote themselves to the end that they all carry in their hearts the death and the bloody sacrifice of the Savior, [and] pray diligently to enter into holiness. And their prayers do not consist of long and empty words, artful phrases and the like; instead, immeasurably more must always be left behind in the heart than one actually says. Prayer is not preaching. We should hourly and moment by moment enter into sincere prayer. And still one thing more. We are priests of the living God. We should daily present our bodies as a sacrifice that is well pleasing to the living, holy God (Romans 12:1). Whoever learns to understand both these acts of worship, whoever can pray and consecrate him or her self to the Lord, will not find it difficult to be a witness of God.

One does not have to think much about it in words because the heart is completely full of the matter. Now and then someone has wanted to prove on the basis of the Christ's high-priestly office that Christians also could teach. But that is not the shortest proof. Priestly lips maintained the doctrine, they were "Custodians of Dogma"; however they were not teaching and preaching the real subject matter.

Witnesses and prophets were distinguished from priests by their call or vocation, when just as many people among the prophets came from priestly lineage as from the nobility and from the very humble. Since it is true that prophetic schools were established in which people were prepared to be teachers. One committed oneself to no tribe, but a priest like Zechariah, a prince like Isaiah, a shepherd like Amos, were all three well trained, thus I speak.

Christians are a people of the [Lord's] possession who are all prophets, and children of the covenant, all appointed to proclaim the virtue of the One who called them (1 Peter 2:9). In the Old Testament such grace and gift is promised to the simplest servant boy or girl (Joel 3:2). But their work does not consist of artful discourses and a gift for analyzing and disentangling subtle questions; rather their work is this: when they come to others they only speak out of the feeling, circumstance, and condition of their souls, which have experienced the Savior, and of the simple and easy way one can and shall acquire this [for oneself].[13]

13. The Count does not reject theological thinking here. He does not say no one should think about subtle or difficult questions. Rather he says that the primary task of a witness of Jesus is not that. The witnesses of Jesus need not be trained theologians, and they need not know the answers to every question. The Count also is not calling for

But when they have experienced [him], they must not say more than they have experienced, and what they know for sure, lest they do harm, and if they want to go further than they themselves already have knowledge, that they would not seduce or tempt by doing so. It is quite edifying when one sees one of these present day prophets and witnesses of the Lord, whose wages are insult, robbery of goods, danger, need and death, and everything a person counts as difficult, and who must struggle against nature. Then one sees that the Lord is true to his servants and they to their Lord,[14] "I would not shun you for the whole world, my Shepherd! Just as from the beginning judgment days and their rewards were not my motivation, that you know" (Jeremiah 17:16).[15]

Children of God! You are anointed, honored people: but cast yourselves at Christ's feet, humble yourselves and bow down; you have grace, you have become his partakers, you have the anointing which is holy and knows all (1 John 2:20).

You people to whom the Savior is still unknown, to whom Jesus is still a stranger: what do you want to understand of him? What name do you carry with you in mortal danger? Since the Lord will not leave unpunished those who misuse his name (Exodus 20:7).

---

people to reduce the Gospel to the content of their own experience or self-consciousness. The Gospel is not a description of my inner states or my experiences. The witness must speak from what they know and must begin with their own experience. But this talk is directed away from itself. The witness points the listener to the Lamb of God, Jesus Christ. Rather than dealing in cold, bloodless abstractions, the witness should speak simply and directly of the Lord and of what the Lord has done.

14. Zinzendorf reshapes the question of truth. It is not a matter of checking for correspondence between some statement and a static state of affairs. Instead, the question of truth is a matter of the trustworthiness and fidelity of this Person. The truth of the Lord is seen in the fact that he remains true to his own and they to him.

15. It is not clear what Zinzendorf is doing here. He is either paraphrasing or interpreting this text from Jeremiah. Or, relying on memory, he may be misquoting the text. But his words are unlike any translation of Jeremiah in either German or English.

The Fourth Speech
(5 March 1738)

True God, Begotten of the Father from Eternity

WE DO NOT WANT TO BE HINDERED BY PROVING THE ETERNAL DEITY of Christ as one might expect here. We only want to recount the details that have become most important and renowned. The innate reason we do not have to get mixed up with such proofs, although ordinarily they appear to be necessary in the highest degree, is that two first principles remove the need for proof.

The first cause which removes the need for demonstration is [this]: [does it not] amount to as much of an absurdity not to believe that if Jesus Christ is God's Son, he is, like his Father, God, as it does to ask whether one who is begotten of a human being, and who everyone sees as the image of his father, who was also identified as such by his father, is also truly a human being? In order to prove that Christ is God one only has to see whether the Holy Spirit names him "Son of God," the One and only begotten Son of God. Accordingly, I once again reiterate without further proof that [Jesus Christ] is just as certainly God because his Father is God, as a human being is human because his father is human.[1]

---

1. Zinzendorf's argument is this:
   1) To have a father is to share the same being as one's father.
   2) Jesus is called the only-begotten Son of God in that he alone among all human beings has God for his own Father, properly speaking.
   3) Therefore, Jesus shares the same being as his Father, the being of God.
   4) Therefore, Jesus is God.
   In Zinzendorf's view, to believe premise 2 but to reject 4 is absurd. To deny 4 is to deny 2 as well.

Therefore one ought not, in fact must not, debate such things. If we still had our wits completely about us [and] had not confounded and pulled apart our God-implanted understanding through over-refinement, so that often the plainest things must be made newly clear to us and a particular discipline (logic) must drive our understanding again into the way, give an account and explain things to those who are students, things which an uneducated boy understands without the slightest explanation and definition if he hears with some attention. It is especially necessary with this holy truth, in which people just wander around so much, that we likewise come back to the vestige of the simple and most natural ideas; in that way it will be revealed consolingly and plainly that [Jesus] is the only-begotten Son of the Father in eternity, coming forth from his heart, just as it is written.

The second reason one should not dispute about the deity of Jesus is this: [one should] avoid all kinds of awkward expressions which do not appear in God's word, which our deficient understanding has to invent first in order to make something plain and articulate it in speech, [avoid] going to that place where a person should not dare to go with his thoughts. He has established the ends of the earth, what is his name and what is his Son's name? Surely you know (Proverbs 30:4)! We do not find this question answered clearly in the Old Testament. But in the New Testament Christ himself answers it (Matthew 11:27; Luke 10:22). "No one knows the Son, except the Father." And thus, we can know nothing about it except what Holy Scripture and he himself says to us, understood in terms of the words themselves, as the words stand, and according to the simplest and most natural way of thinking God bestows upon us. With such simplicity of faith and certainty we are entirely confident, we stand fast and require nothing more to demonstrate this secret. As it stands written, so one reads it.

To be sure, before we proceed to the matter, we presuppose something that must be offered as an apology to those who begin to feel uneasy with their thoughts about the deity of Christ because they are not able to set forth a proof against the adversaries. Nevertheless, they mean no harm, but were only led by the arguments that demonstrate the Messianic office of the Savior, to prove that he is God by virtue of his origin. These are certainly two completely distinct ideas. Without doubt one cannot and must not prove the deity [of the Son] by means of the arguments Christ and the apostles used to prove that he is the promised

Messiah and the anointed One of God.[2] Therefore it certainly will not do at all to want sayings that deal with the circumstances of [his] abasement and adoption of human nature to prove his sovereign deity [[in the fullness of time, when he was looked upon as a laborer of God, as a servant in the house of God, when he himself was one of the hired hands and only the first and highest among them, according to which circumstances the Father is clearly greater than he is, and it was good to grant him to remember, John 14:28, that he was returning to the Father to enter again into his former unity with him from which he hitherto had not gained a thing: "Father, transfigure me with your brightness, which I shared with you before the world was."]][3]

As for the rest, it is easy thanks to the [reasons] cited here to deconstruct why the talk is so varied [in the New Testament] and Christ is sometimes described as inferior to the Father but sometimes [as] equal to him. Since it remains fixed that the Word who once became flesh lived like any other person in lowliness and poverty, even as a servant, who to be sure had precedence over all others in God's house but who was like his brothers in all details except sin, and all his speeches themselves establish his inner and hidden magnificence, but in the most scrupulous concealment, and while he was omnipresent at that time he never gave [it] away plainly by [his sayings];[4] thus it

2. In other words, to confess that Jesus is the Christ, God's anointed, is separate and different from confessing that he is God. It is logically possible to believe that Jesus is the Christ and not to believe that he is God incarnate, as the Ebionites and Arians did in ancient times. Therefore, Zinzendorf considers it a mistake in reasoning to try to use arguments that Jesus is the Christ to prove that he shares the being of God. That calls for other arguments.

3. This section in double brackets was not part of the speeches as Zinzendorf originally presented them. He added this to the published version.

4. According to Zinzendorf, who here offers a deeply Lutheran reading of the Christian tradition, the New Testament sometimes describes Jesus as inferior to the Father because in his full humanity he is always God *incognito*. Even in revelation God remains the *Deus absconditus*, the hidden God. Even in revelation God remains mysterious and elusive, never subject to our categories or controls. Zinzendorf even maintains that Jesus continued to be omnipresent during his incarnation. This is an expression of the Lutheran christological doctrine of the *communicatio idiomatum* (the doctrine that says that the union of the two natures in Christ is such that properties of deity are transferred to his humanity so that, for example, after the resurrection the body of Jesus Christ can be said to be ubiquitous. It is an assertion of the full unity of the person of the Savior. If Jesus is present now, it is exactly the same one who is present to us as was present to the disciples in the hills of Galilee). Here Zinzendorf wants to

is absolutely necessary to dissociate oneself from all arguments which prove the sovereign majesty of his humanity, according to which he is at all times half of the official position [of God] and under God.[5] On the contrary, one must ponder in an even more heartfelt manner that out of love for us the Father gave up his Son in the form of sinful flesh, and thereby surrendered himself not only to send his Son but even to subordinate him to the law, and in case he wanted to be self-satisfied, that [the Son] might ultimately taste death for us all (the only exception was decomposition, because he could not resolve to do that). It remains to be said that it is impossible for us to know the Savior's divinity and its depths; we neither can nor should know it: to be sure we are also to take comfort that he revealed it to us as much as he wills (Matthew 11:27). Without doubt this verdict of the matter is determined by the criterion. "A servant does not know what his master is doing; but I have said that you are my friends" (John 15:15).

The very same One who would not allow a teacher of the Jews to call him "good," because [the teacher] did not believe him to be God and no one except God is good; this One on another occasion accepted worship from a man born blind and made no objection to it. If he had not in the same way gladly made his deity clear, then he likewise could absolutely not contest it but in fact sometimes received and accepted worship, which otherwise belongs to God alone. He was simply unvarnished truth. It was he himself who so ordered things that baptism should take place not merely in the name of the Father and of the Holy Spirit, but also in his name. John fell at his feet like a dead man (Revelation 1:17), and Jesus made no objection to it as did the great angel twice [when John fell at his feet] (Revelation 19:10; 22:9). "Do not do this; I am your fellow servant and your brother, and brother of all those who have the testimony of Jesus," [said the angel]. And because

---

say as forcefully as possible that even in his abasement and humiliation, or precisely in these, the Son did not cease being the One who gives light and life to all things.

5. This is a rejection of subordinationism in all its forms, whether in the ancient form of Arius or the modern forms of the Enlightenment and Romanticism. The Son is never "under," or subjected to, God in Zinzendorf's way of thinking. The Christian must necessarily take the entire testimony of the New Testament seriously. Therefore, the Christian must learn to live, think, and speak within the dialectical tension between a confession of Jesus' full and authentic humanity on the one hand, and the confession of his full and authentic deity on the other. Any nondialectical understanding of Jesus Christ is, in the end, not Christian.

he well knew that all the angels of God must worship him he could not at all directly spoil the mind and inclination of his children to worship him. But he gave us understanding so that we know to respect him, so that nothing is taken away from love. "He raised his hands and blessed them, and when he had blessed them he departed from them and went into heaven; but they worshiped him." That was one example [of this inclination to worship him]; and it was a natural consequence of the solemnity. The second [example] was even more natural; following him with their eyes, the painful, loving, longing gaze. "Now do not be so sad," the angel said, "You will see him again; but you need not think that you will become unaccustomed [to seeing him], he will show himself to you again, just as you have known him."

Now we want to make several observations about the divinity of the Savior that crop up in the Holy Scriptures. First, Christ is the only One in the bosom of the Father (John 1:14, 18). Second, since those [others] called "Children of God" are only children by adoption, elected by grace, and not simply at the time when Christ died, which was the seal and completion of our election, but rather they are already elected at creation, indeed since before the foundation of the world: but all for the sake of Christ, the only-begotten Son of God, and on account of the particular relationship with him. That makes us belong to the family of God and it is given us by grace to be called God's children (John 1:12). But Jesus Christ is by authority and rights, by birth and by nature, a Son of God, originating from the [Father's] heart.

It follows from the second observation that the Father loves the Son by nature. After all, after [Jesus'] baptism [the Father] said, "You are my dear Son, you are all my delight, in whom I have all my enjoyment." That is the secret of the love between the Son and the Father, which overflowed in [Jesus'] last prayer (John 17). The Father also bears public witness to the love he has for the Son, that he is of one heart and will with him, that the word and the being of Father and Son have a single purpose, vigor, and power. The Father spoke with us through the only Son, who is in the bosom of the Father, who explained to us what the Father does and purposes.

God's love for Christ cannot be altered or reduced (John 3:35), but rather it remains eternally and changelessly and the Father embraces the Son with a sweet, hearty, and inexpressible tenderness, of which no one has a complete grasp except the Spirit, who searches out the depths of the

Deity (1 Corinthians 2:10). We (his souls) cannot interfere on account of our humanity and the weakness of our understanding: but rather if we have perceived something of his love we simply think, "If this [partial perception] is already so excellent, how must [the full reality] be!"

The third observation concerning the Son in relation to the Father is that the Father did not spare his only begotten and affectionately loved Son, but gave him up for us all (Romans 8:32). God loved the world thus, that he gave his only-begotten Son in order that whoever believes on him should not be lost, but have everlasting life (John 3:16). This shows a depth in God's love, this proves a fatherly heart, (a universal heart) which wills to be merciful to all, since the heart takes the counsel of the Deity to be true, indeed to be invariably necessary for poor human beings, and saw or knew apart from this no other way: a person sharing in the divine being had to give himself to reconcile the world with himself, that the Father, in order to become the caretaker of humanity, and to experience our need, filth and dirt, poverty and death, granted his fatherly blessing to the Son [saying]: "Go forth, valued Crown of my heart and be the salvation of the poor and helpless."

The fourth point is that the Father did not force the Son to suffer; rather it was a free decision of this sovereign-divine person himself. The Father did not persuade the Son through argument [to the effect that] he would be crowned with praises and honor afterwards, and if he would just pass through the process of suffering and place himself in the lower level [of being] and lay down his life so that he could take it up again, then his situation would be even more Lordly. One can imagine such a motive in the case of an angel or a human being, and the latter not even based on the New Testament; but in the case of a Person [who participates] in the Deity, who was in the bosom of the Father before the foundation of the world, the alleging of such an argument would be a blasphemous ridicule. He had the power to lay down his life.

He was not made nor did he come into existence in order to redeem humanity and at the same time have the capacity to refuse to burden himself with the wrath of God. If he had not wished it himself, then he could have refrained from doing it at any time. He would always continue to be God, and we would be the devil's laughing stock. It was exclusively up to him, and if he begged his Father on the Mount of Olives that the Father might take a bitter cup away from him; [[because this form of fearfulness, confusion, darkness, and inner perplexity also had to become a part of him so that he would know how a wavering person feels and be able to help such a person by virtue of his own experience (Hebrews 2:17–18)]];[6] thus the saying [on the Mount of Olives] was not about suffering and dying, but rather about the ghastly anguish of atonement and death by which he had to grapple, pray, sweat, and charm sin and death away so that they [sin and death] lay like a whole world upon his human shoulders.[7] But after [this prayer] he explained regarding suffering and dying that he only had to say a single word to his Father and plenty of angels would be at the ready [to rescue him]; but he had come to this hour in order to suffer. He remained the sovereign Lord, doing and suffering whatever he willed right into the pit; but his love drove him through the entire struggle to victory.

The fifth venerable observation is that the Father loved him for this reason, that he gave his life (John 10:17), that he humbled himself unto death, in fact, the death of the cross. Therefore, the Father already looked upon his intention with delight; and afterwards, when he had won through the process, when all was well accomplished, the guarantee [of salvation] arranged, when the world had been bought, how the Father's heart rejoiced over the completion! The Son is to him now the most beloved man.

The sixth salient point is that the Father appointed a recompense to the beloved man for all the effort and work he would have in the world. Therefore, because his soul toiled, he shall see his delight and be satisfied. He shall deliver humanity and shall bring one after another into glory. The recompense which he accepts as a man is also an example of the reward of his followers who conquer after him, and who shall take their seat with him in his glory (Revelation 3), but he can have no greater joy and consolation in his poor ones than the multitude of souls.[8]

6. Zinzendorf added the passage within the double brackets for the published version of the speeches.

7. Zinzendorf frequently uses the classical, or *Christus Victor*, model of the atonement (cf., Aulen, *Christus Victor*). This model is very dramatic. Its central theme is that in Christ God descends into the abyss and fights on our behalf against all the dark powers of the devil, death, and hell. He triumphs over them all and invites us to participate in his victory.

8. In other words, the only reward the Savior desires and seeks is that people should come to him and be rescued. His delight is in his people, the community of those who belong to him and to each other in him.

He is the Lord over all and the Creator of the world (Hebrews 1:8, 10). Judgment has been turned over to him (John 5:27). All the glory and majesty of the throne of the kingly reign of Jesus belongs to the humanity (Matthew 28:18).[9] And that is the only possible sense of the words: "The Son will become subject to . . ." (1 Corinthians 15:28).[10] If [these words] are to have a meaning which is not contrary to every pronouncement of all the prophets and apostles up to the Savior himself, that his kingly reign shall have no end, which [phrase] the dear, blessed confessors of Augsburg quite earnestly adopted.[11]

Because here in the reign of grace he is the true servant of God, the householder in charge of God's house, the head of the body, the judge of his witnesses, indeed the duke of their struggles and victories; thus he cannot always remain the servant and laborer, but the economy[12] is not complete until his final enemy lies as a footstool under his feet. The last enemy to be dealt with is death.

The Savior himself says that a servant does not retain his function forever (John 8:35). But the Son remains always in the house, "In the house, that is never deserted and never dies out, and where there is no succession [of leaders]."[13] [The Savior's] humanity and servant hood possesses a level of great importance. He increased in wisdom, seniority, and grace. If he lacked knowledge of something, he learned it; he

9. This is an explicit statement of Zinzendorf's Lutheran *communicatio idiomatum* Christology.

10. The Count thinks that Paul's words must be taken to mean something like that Jesus' humanity was subject to the Father, but not the Savior himself in his divine/human unity. The Son is never subordinated to the Father.

11. This is a reference to the Augsburg Confession, located in the *Book of Concord*.

12. "Economy" (Greek *oikonomia*) was the word the ancient teachers of the Christian movement used to describe the whole narrative of God's salvation in history. The term comes from the ordering or managing of a household. Paul used it to describe God's plan and care for the whole creation. Ancient Christian teachers used it to sum up the central events that reveal God's gracious will toward us. Thus, it referred to the events of Jesus' incarnation, his words and deeds, and his suffering, death, and resurrection. In this way God's economy was sharply distinguished from speculation about God. All talk about God that is not about these events constitutes empty prattling or human projecting. True talk about God must be talk about God's economy, which is to say, about Jesus in his life, suffering, death, and resurrection from the dead.

13. Zinzendorf quotes a hymn. It rhymes in German and is shorter. But the German phrase bears a double meaning which I have incorporated into my translation. The German phrase means both that the house will never be deserted, and that it will never die out. Moreover, the Savior never ceases being its Master and Leader.

prayed and was heard. It is settled then, that the majesty he had before the foundation of the world is to be sharply distinguished from the humiliation he allowed himself to experience out of love, even though [this refers] simply [to] the man Jesus Christ, and he is only one Christ. But who can understand this, as can the one to whom the Son of Man reveals it? Such a wise one keeps silent, hears, and worships him and says, "Amen," to his deity and humanity.

So that is that, Jesus Christ is God over all highly praised in eternity (Romans 9:5), and he emptied himself out of love for us, and gave expression to his glory. Jesus Christ is exactly the same yesterday and today as he is in the eternities of eternities (Hebrews 13:8).[14] "Angels and people look upon him with inexpressible joy."[15]

He grants us who have here and there heard of his redemption to bow before him in the time of grace, and allows us to become his members, his very own flesh and bone according to the humanity, but he remains the head of the body, which is the community. Who would not want out of love for him to throw away with a thousand joys many small things of the world, which our corrupt reason and seductive hearts hold up, and to live to him alone? Let us never wander from these two considerations. First: that God was a guest in the world, nevertheless without sin, indeed he was just as poverty stricken as we poor people are; because that makes us willing and able to become a reward for his effort and work.

The second thing is that our Brother, our Savior who is loved in a heartfelt manner, the Reconciler of sinners, the Lover of humanity who took on the form of a poor servant, is no less God the Lord in the heights. This makes the prophets speak of the whole world as a tiny speck of dust and the nations as a drop of water from a bucket. It makes it sometimes seem absolutely as if we and our Lord were alone in the world, and we simply stop being amazed, experiencing sadness, and taking pleasure; because he becomes to us predominant over all.

14. Zinzendorf here translates the Greek phrase literally. In English the phrase is customarily translated as "forever."

15. Once again, a hymn text helps Zinzendorf say Christian teaching.

The Fifth Speech
(9 March 1738)

Truly Human, Born in Time of the Virgin Mary

THE FATHER ALSO PLACED JUDGMENT IN HIS HANDS, BECAUSE HE IS A "Son of Man," a human being. These are the Savior's own words about himself in John 5:27, in which he makes himself plain concerning this great secret.

The cause of his becoming human, as everyone knows, is that no one could reconcile God; no brother, no angel, no creature; thus *Jehovah*,[1] the Creator of all things, desired to restore human creatures, and the Father gave his only-begotten Son for us all. Of course, God could not die, and he willed to die. Therefore, he emptied himself and took the form of a servant (Philippians 2:7), the form of sinful flesh (Romans 8:3), and became as truly human as he was God. So as he was formerly in the form of God, one saw him afterwards in human form, just as truly human in human form as he whom the angels of God had worshiped in the original divine form. That is why we, if we on the one hand cast ourselves into the dust at his feet because he is God, the Lord most high, we also on the other hand draw near to him with joy, affection, and full confidence because he is completely human just like us.

---

1. This was for a long time a common way among Christians to render the four-consonant Hebrew name of God. We now know that it is an incorrect vocalization. Some, including some scholars, now use *Yahweh* in its place. It seems better for theological, linguistic, and religious reasons to continue to follow Jewish tradition and refrain from trying to pronounce the name. One should simply say "Lord" instead.

I am being long winded, but not without reason, because so very many only pay attention to the historical concept of this truth. Since to believe firmly that God became a human being and tasted death for us, as one can say of several other matters truthfully and honestly that one believes them; that is the true means for us to be saved all at once. We require no more. Because the Gospel, that is, the account that Jesus came into the world and lived among us, including the simple stories, how he died, is a power of God to save all who believe (Romans 1:16). Every spirit that confesses that Jesus came in the flesh is from God (1 John 4:3). No one is able to call Jesus "Lord," (which refers to our situation, when he is our Lord as the Son of Man), except through the Holy Spirit (1 Corinthians 12:3).

Imagine everyone who in actuality believes as a Gospel that the Son of God became a human being and wandered in the world for thirty years, for the good of all, but especially for those who believe it, and finally endured the most despised death sentence, by comparison hanging is still acceptable in certain lands; should they not by means of this get such an impression as they can never forget? There are plenty of examples of people receiving such an impression from humble events that they remember it their whole life long.[2] One sees by looking at them [that] from the very hour they have not been the same. Therefore, one has a habit of saying about many people who had thought to be seen as solitary, who do not enjoy people's physical company, "From that time on they were never again joyful." How much more is it a divine certainty that one who believes that Christ died, who sees his bloody form hanging in Spirit, cannot remain indifferent, if he has an otherwise reasonable soul that is not brought into insanity through desires. If he appears in the same form as when he so generously bled to death upon the cross for our need, and one holds it to be no fantasy, and allows oneself not to be talked out of it again; then one keeps an abiding memory of him which one never forgets as long as one lives; either fearfully and desolately if one does not take it completely into one's heart, or

---

2. Zinzendorf has in mind here ordinary and mundane experiences that take on a profound impact and meaning. He always remembered the first time he participated in Holy Communion. Although it seemed quite ordinary to everyone around him, he later said that something happened to him in it that stayed with him his whole life long. The ordinary and everyday can suddenly become unveiled as the bearer of God's mysterious presence and grace.

happily, indeed [in] abundant happiness, if one from then on fruitfully bears in mind this death and its cause.

Therefore, this is the work of the witnesses of Jesus when they speak with people: to preach the crucified Savior into their hearts and to paint him before their eyes, just as he once truly died and was dead; whether he now likewise lives from eternity to eternity and holds the keys of death and hell. Paul showed his wisdom, his great wisdom, in that among the Corinthians he knew and preached nothing except Jesus, and him crucified (1 Corinthians 2:2). This matter has since become scorned, because it has so often been sung, prayed, and taught without understanding so that the teacher did not know anymore what he was saying and the hearer did not know what he should think. So through habit and abuse this secret of godliness has degenerated into foolishness. But whoever is intelligent, or whoever, as Paul says, is perfectly clever according to human wisdom, to that person it is surely wisdom (1 Corinthians 2:6). Therefore we want to press this matter as much to the forefront as the Lord gives us grace to do.

One other benefit of the future of Christ in the flesh is that he is able to judge. He knows how we are feeling (Hebrews 2:14–18). He can have patience with us and understands where lukewarmness and weakness part company.[3] He felt our affliction because he was truly human according to soul and body just as all the children have flesh and blood. Consequently, we must view him as a faithful high priest, and believe that he was, in every detail and in poverty of the deepest self and in all other circumstances under which his children still now wallow,[4] like us during the time he spent on earth. He experienced everything [his people] can meet with in life. He became like the absolute lowest and least. There is no person in such a wretched shape and form who should not be able to remember and find comfort in that Jesus was at one time exactly like him.

---

3. Zinzendorf's point is that the Savior knows the depths of our consciousness better than we ourselves. The Savior knows the difference between our personal weakness, our ignorance, and our failure because of sin on the one hand, and callous indifference on the other. Zinzendorf wants to comfort sinners with the thought that the Savior knows our weaknesses and loves and forgives us in them.

4. Zinzendorf uses the French verb *croupir* and adds the grammatically correct German ending.

His whole suffering, death, and justification in his own person, through which he paid the penalty for Adam's fall, was no illustration, sham fight, and work of deception, but rather it was severe truth. In the desert he experienced the assaults of the devil, indeed the fiery attacks of the evil one. He battled as a man and had recourse to God's word and to prayer, just like other children of God. He persevered in unwavering abandonment to and faith in his Father. [When] he went hungry for forty days, he experienced a great weakness of the deepest self and whatever else a human being can encounter in such circumstances. Nevertheless he had the power of his eternal deity (which he seemed to have left alone, Matthew 27:46, and was ranked under the angels, Hebrews 2:9) for relief in the state of affairs in which we now need him and have him at our side, just as he had his and our God at his side at that time. Therefore it happens that the Savior in his humiliation says: "My Father and your Father, your God and my God." From this proceed the sayings of Christ that several who prefer not to believe that he is the eternal God bring so diligently against his deity, but [these sayings] prove as badly that he is not God just as badly as they prove that he is (as others wish to do). He held his dominion secretly and could not allow his disciples to divulge it, if they became aware of something special in him; and when they saw him transfigured he wanted them to say nothing to others about it. He well knew that people were not inclined to believe in him for that reason.[5] They could not grasp that a person must be born of the Spirit, how much more would they be astounded and bewildered if he had spoken about the depths of his deity (John 3:12)? That is the reason why many of his disciples turned away when he explained clearly about the effects and particulars of his divine nature (John 6:66).

Therefore, it proves nothing against the Savior and is foolishness to quote such expressions that speak of the time of his humiliation. If a person were in the most extreme distress, anguish, and abasement of the deepest self, and said: "I am a worm, a useless creature," etc., exactly as several precious witnesses of Jesus behaved at their ends, and one wanted to close the books, as though they were in fact just that, and had done nothing in the world; that would be a completely foolish conclusion.

---

5. That is to say, people did not come to trust the Savior because they first became convinced of his deity. Knowledge of his deity was (and is) not the cause of faith.

The face of Moses shone and he didn't know it (Exodus 34:29). It re-
dounds to the glory of the witnesses that they regard themselves so
humbly, when they are so important to the Lord and to people. "I know
your poverty, but you are rich" (Revelation 2:9). "So if I honor myself,"
says the Savior, "My honor is nothing" (John 8:54). "The time is already
come that you see who I am and what you had in me." It was not of the
Savior's cause. He did not please himself (Romans 15:3). "When your
Comforter (Isaiah 66:13) the Holy Spirit comes, that One will explain
everything to you" (John 16:13).

As we now indisputably know that he is God; so must we also
believe that he is a human being just like us, (exactly like us) flesh of
our flesh and bone of our bone. It follows necessarily from this (as our
catechism states) that we believe his word through his grace and live
a godly life, just as he [did] in time and [does] eternally. If we took it
to the highest level, indeed we know that we are human beings; he the
householder, we the servants; he the Son in the house, we the adopted
children; he God, we his creatures; we members, he the head: he has life
in himself, we have it from him. We have everything from his grace and
mercy. This point stands fast: with respect to worthiness we are nothing
in relation to him, little specks of dust and not even to be taken into
consideration. We have all grace, strength, virtues and gifts from him.

In spite of this we become, as he was. We can believe, we can
love, we can preserve faith and good conscience, like him. In his last
Testament he even requested and got it for us from the Father, that he
might be in us and we in him and that the Father should look after us
(John 17:15; 21, 23). That is a matter of greatest importance and should
make an impression in all hearts. It should be a joy to us to tread in his
footsteps and to walk as he walked. "Since we have such hope in him,
we purify ourselves, just as he is pure" (1 John 3:3), and "whoever says
they abide in him should walk as he walked" (1 John 2:6).

But with that we do not tumble into self-chosen duties and self-
righteous holiness, but rather remain with the chief work, that Jesus
Christ was a man and only thus accordingly narrate the gospel history;
so we only still have to ask ourselves whether the matter is not important and everything depends on it. Whether or not salvation and all else
depends on our knowing positively that Jesus was a man. The answer is:
Jesus is as much a human being as we are; thus people bore witness to
us who can communicate nothing else to us (even if they testified in the

clearest, most inward and best conveyance of the heart, and have given their children up to God from the mother's womb on) except what they themselves had by nature and from grace, namely that they are human beings, with an attestation both of sinfulness and grief and of the comfort of grace. Spiritual death, which all human seed carries within itself, must first be overpowered through the death of Jesus Christ, our life be buried in his death, and re-animated by his life, when we reach many years and old age. Our wretchedness is present as long as we are here in this life, and the occasions for failure that present themselves are often a whetstone on which our loyalty to him is sharpened. To be sure, all soldiers of Christ have everything they need in order not to allow that which is not good in them to rule them, but rather to conquer it.

In one respect the Savior is different [from us]. He was from the Holy Spirit, and how could it be otherwise? Otherwise he would also have been a sinner by nature, and would not have been able to redeem us. The depth of the reality demanded that God's Son stride into the middle, and [that] the eternal Word had to suffer in his human body what we have to suffer; do what we have to do; and experience what we experience. Without the eternal Word, through which all things are made and without which nothing can exist, there could also exist no eternal reconciliation.

We can learn from this what sin and evil might be like, so that humans put forth a lot of effort and so that the casuists make a lot of effort where they do not have to. The case with the life of the Savior will decide that immediately. All afflictions that do not hinder the relation of the person to God as child to parent, we find in the Savior. We come across him tired, afraid, hungry and thirsty, and in situations when he didn't know any way out and [how] to help himself, in ignorance of such things as it seemed good for him to know; therefore he said, when his disciples asked him about a certain period of time: He did not know, his Father in heaven alone knew it (Matthew 24:36); and when two of them desired to sit one on his right and the other on his left, he said that wasn't up to him, but rather to his Father in heaven (Matthew 20:23). When his disciples were with him on the Mount of Olives and slept on account of their need, sadness, and confusion; the Savior reminded them three times, as if it was really important to him, and was becoming melancholy in his heart of hearts over the fact that they didn't stay awake. Where a servant of Jesus is weak in the inner self and does things which do not come from the heart but from a self overstrained by suffering and distress; there the example of the Savior is a comfort. Everything that human nature and [the] soul can encounter, which is not against its meaning and against the nature of a soul that is redeemed by Jesus, but [reflects] rather only poverty and powerlessness, and is a proof that a lot is still lacking, which one would gladly have, and would be necessary, yes, even fear, [all this] we find in the Savior; and that should be our establishment[6] in sufferings and training exercises. It is the highest necessity that we not deny the Savior's imperfection, defeatedness, and misery, or seek other secrets in them than that they are meritorious, and we should rightly consider his patience and his end (James 5:11).[7] If we know what became of the Lord Jesus, into what shame, distressed circumstances and conflicts he fell before God and humanity; then this can serve as an encouragement to us gladly to be wretched and forsaken.

But everything which he did not commit, and what he did not do, not so much because it was against his Office and Rank as that it was contrary to the will of his Father, we should and can also refrain from doing. This is the mirror of holiness: "We have the mind of Christ" (1 Corinthians 2:16). We cannot acquire this mind other than by being reminded that the high and lofty One, who lives eternally (Isaiah 57:15), allowed himself to come down and appeared in the form of sinful flesh, and in his own body judged, damned, and paid the penalty for sin. Whoever thinks about this seriously and can truly affirm this one thing: "Jesus had to suffer until body and soul separated," constantly as that upon which his heart rests, that person has a foundation laid in Christ upon which he or she can build everything that should be built as long as he or she is here in preparation. Everything must be grounded upon the knowledge of Jesus' incarnation; thereafter it is worth the effort to place the gold, silver and precious stones of the virtues upon it. "No one can lay another foundation" (1 Corinthians 3:11).

We want to become perfect, not that we become the holiest people and leave all sin behind, (since that is correspondingly a trifling matter for the One who dwells in us) but rather in the sense in which Paul

---

6. That is, our solid rock, our strong foundation, our mighty fortress.

7. Jesus' "end" is what happened to him in the world, namely, his rejection, arrest, torture, and murder.

speaks of perfection (Philippians 3:15), in that way we have to learn the secret.*

Now this is the great secret of true religion: God is revealed in the flesh. This is the prize, (the treasure) of which Paul wanted to take hold, namely to know him and the power of his resurrection and the fellowship of, that is to take part in, his agony and merit. And when Paul says "Fight the good fight of faith, become lord over sin, the world, and the devil"; then he says at the same time, "Take hold of eternal life" (1 Timothy 6: 12). This belongs also to eternal life: to learn to know Jesus Christ (John 17:3). And John wrote this to his own so that their joy might be complete (1 John 1:4).

Here [in this life] it is a matter of patchwork, where we do not know everything; but there [in the resurrection, the fullness of God's reign] it is [the] perfect condition when we know him just as we are known (1 Corinthians 13:12). Therefore, religion is not a matter of our knowing everything in a systematic and orderly manner, but rather that we allow ourselves day by day to be initiated more [deeply] into this subject: that Jesus out of grace was a human being like us, and exactly like us, and that it can and must also be said of us, "As he is, so are we in this world" (1 John 4:17).

---

* [Zinzendorf added the following note to the published edition of the speeches.] In spite of the one hundred and eighty fifth question put forth by A. G. Spangenberg in *The Exposition*, through this construction apparently almost removed, we want to set forth here an explanation with the answer:

Question: A certain theologian writes, "Do you [Zinzendorf] not have little regard for true salvation and godliness, since you said in the *Berlin Speeches*: "To become a holy person and leave all sin behind is only a little thing?"

Answer: As soon as all the holiness and blessedness of the angels comes to stand in us over against the revelation of Christ; this holiness [apart from Christ himself] is, as the Halle Brethren sing, darkness. [[Translator's note: Zinzendorf's point, of course, is that his only righteousness is Jesus Christ himself. It is, therefore, in the deepest sense external to him. It is not his own production or possession. He wants no other righteousness, godliness, or salvation than simply Christ himself.]]

The Sixth Speech
(12 March 1738)

My Lord

MY LORD AND MY GOD, YOU KNOW THE BLESSEDNESS ONE HAS IN THE knowledge that you are one's Father, and how one is suddenly snatched away from all the calamitous circumstances which one had in one's former freedom of the flesh. You know, O King of the whole world, how good the free people of your house and your servants have it, who give themselves to you willingly, who therefore beseech you that you would be willing to deem them worthy of your commands and supreme sovereignty. Make us all so blessed, we who are here in your presence, and permit what this important and extraordinary truth contains within itself, if not with the exact precision which would be necessary for it, still to be testified to in accordance with the truth, for the sake of your grace, Amen.

"So all who do not love the Lord Jesus, let them be damned" (1 Corinthians 16:22). This word of the apostle Paul's follows the greetings that he gives to souls. On account of this connection it appears as if an anathema were pronounced upon all the members of the community who do not love Jesus, because it stands [for] the opposite of the church greeting which in ancient times had more meaning than it does today. Since it is well known that John refuses the greeting to the anti-Christs, who deny the deity of Christ (2 John, verse 10). Now when Paul directs the community to greet and moreover adds to what he said: "I Paul greet you with my own hand"; he makes an exception of those who do not love Jesus, [even] if they might equally belong to the crowd.

But I do not want to linger over whether it might be a formula of excommunication or only an account of the disastrous situation of souls who do not love Jesus, as in Revelation 21:11.[1] "Whoever is wicked, is after all wicked; whoever is righteous may abide so," that accordingly he says here: "Whoever does not love the Lord Jesus is precisely accursed," cannot inherit the blessing, cannot even be helped, our peace cannot rest upon such a one; because the cause of all peace is Christ, our Peace. So let it be to one as one wants, although the expression undergoes modification, the import of the thing still remains, which declared that all souls of a community who do not love Jesus Christ are damned. Because one must make a distinction (in accordance with the Gospel) between people who have heard nothing of Jesus and have not made their way into his communion, and people who think it necessary to be in a society which is assembled in the name of Jesus.

All sayings, all threats, all admonitions of the apostle refer to the present time. Everybody wants to put on a frame of mind that they never possessed, it cannot be helped, out of which conclusions emerge which were completely contrary to the apostle's intention. They have not abandoned their general plan to request humbly for all people to be devoted to the Lord Jesus. They have not pronounced their ban over people who have nothing to do with them. [Yet] they have never once acted with zeal concerning those who were not in the community, but have only ever dealt seriously with people over whom they had power to command; as Paul expresses twice, first to Timothy, "I order you before God" (1 Timothy 6:13), second to the Thessalonians, "We command you in the name of our Lord Jesus Christ" (2 Thessalonians 3:6), which formula he explains to Philemon, "I have the power to command you"; and that is therefore the manner of the servants of God, because when one says to people who have experienced nothing of grace and strength what they should do, how they should show themselves, it is just as if one were to give the job of message carrier to a paralyzed person or wanted a blind person to pass judgment on all sorts of things for which sharp eyesight is demanded. "Whoever despises the poor, sneers at his Creator" (Proverbs 17:5).[2]

---

1. Zinzendorf gives the reference as chapter 21, but it is actually in chapter 22.

2. Zinzendorf criticizes the church here. "They" continue to pray for those outside the community of disciples, those who do not know Jesus. But they do not lift a finger to do anything for them. "They" (the church) only has to do with those they can order

Whoever causes natural people, who do not have Jesus in their hearts, indeed who cannot have him, who are often hindered by many other things, to have merely a proper concept of Jesus, will, considered in the abstract, damn himself; that person presumes a vast matter which is not his duty. It is not the job of a witness of Jesus to proclaim judgment over people; he must first know who he has in front [of him]. Therefore, though in relation to us so-called Christians, who attend to the form of biblical religion, and would rather not have it said to us, that we do not belong to the house of God, to the Church of Jesus Christ, the method of threat, that which the apostle says, could be explained quite justly; thus must I freely confess, that in that way, the old corruption, which we have by nature, which should be taken from us after baptism according to our doctrine, and even can actually have been taken away, is back again. It is no longer a threat, but rather with most among us is a fact of reality, that "You do not love the Lord Jesus."

The great claim that the Savior has on our love is based upon various truths of Holy Scripture. In Psalm 110 it says, "After your triumph your people will be genuinely ready." That explains Isaiah chapter 53:11–12. "Because his soul labored, he will see his delight and have abundance. For this reason he shall get a great throng as booty." But the apostle draws the conclusion, and explains it as clearly as the sun and undeniably as far as the just person is concerned, when he says, "For this reason he died for all, so that those who live might from now on live not for themselves but rather for the One who died and rose again" (2 Corinthians 5:15), and in another place, "For this Christ died and rose and lives again, that he might be Lord both of the dead and of the living" (Romans 14:9). Therefore to him belongs the rule and the scepter over all souls, over all people on the whole expanse of the earth, particularly over those who are in a society, who are in a crowd or community where his teaching is freely spoken, is publicly testified to and certified, on account of which they are distinguished from unbelievers, where they speak to the Jews dwelling every day in their presence, and want to appear before them, as if they were people who had taken Jesus

---

around. And if they try to give orders to people who are not Christians, they do evil. It is unreasonable and wicked to command people to do something they simply cannot, something for which they lack the capacity because they do not live by faith. To expect people who are not Christians to live as though they were Christians is, as the Count says, to sneer at their Creator.

of Nazareth as their Lord and God, whom the former did not know. But one asks: "In what shall his Lordship consist?" Answer: "In that his people are ready and willing to serve him with delight and joy." The Savior bears witness to this with the words, "Whoever loves me will keep my word" (John 14:23), and the converse, "Why do you call me Lord and not do what I say?" (Luke 6:46).

The beginning is not to make an effort to do what the Savior commanded. For, as has been said many times already, [those] who begin with actions when they are still powerless in spirit, when they are still dead, when they are still blind, when they still have no grace, when they have not yet experienced the power of God, but instead still stand in their own power; they are ready for absolutely nothing: and when they do something, they make a fabric which is worthless. [They have] a foundation whose superficiality [they] will not see and notice, but in the meantime [they] sink ever deeper into ruin, the more they have confidence in the foundation. We can give nothing, we must first have. We must have grace, forgiveness in the blood of Jesus. We must first know why he is Lord of us and of the whole world, so that each soul must experience purely as such, why he is Lord. Each soul must be able to say with joy: "He is my Lord."

What Thomas said, when [the Savior's] stripes, his wounds, his nail-holes, his pierced side were presented to him, which was absolutely to be distinguished from that which on the Day of Judgment either the nations and peoples of the earth will all do, or to be sure the main body of the people who took responsibility upon themselves for his innocently shed blood: "They will see him whom they pierced, and will howl." Thomas said, "My Lord and my God." That was the effect of the look that he took of the nail-holes. On account of that he knew that Jesus is his Lord; he also confessed that in his person the prophet's saying was fulfilled, that "His people will offer themselves to him willingly" (Psalm 110). He was the first among the disciples who did what Mary Magdalene, the great sinner, was first among all people to do, to fall at his feet and recognize him. Afterwards all the disciples did it—fell before him and worshiped him.

Undoubtedly the word that Christ is Lord is of extraordinary extension, experience and power. Whoever in the present wicked world knows that Jesus is his Lord has discovered a secret that constantly comforts and heartens in every situation, every day of life, and in everything that can befall a person. It is not a difficult matter; and because it is an easy thing, it is an even greater sign of the corruption, damnation, and death of a soul, if one cannot say, "He is my Lord." Since to have Jesus for one's Lord is nothing other than that one is convinced in one's soul, "He has proved a faithfulness to me, which I have experienced from no one in the whole world, and [I] can thank him in no other way than with my very self." What no angel, no human being, not the highest-ranking friend, not the mightiest patron, and not the greatest possible protector can by any means do for me, he has accomplished. And the faithfulness that he has done for us, he continues as long as he lives, but he dies nevermore. "Christ rose from the dead, and will never die again" (Romans 6:9). We know, whether we live in time or in eternity, we keep this Lord.

We will also not go out of his service; it goes well for us eternally in his house. We have a friendly Master, and when we go wrong in something on account of our poverty and incompetence, then he will always pass judgment on us according to our hearts, and never require of us the result of the thing, but rather only [what] was intended [by us]. The greatest deeds without heart do not convince the Savior that a person belongs to him. To move mountains, to drive out devils, to heal the sick, does not mean that he acknowledges us as his own. For when people will say on that day, "Lord, have we not prophesied in your name, have we not driven out devils in your name, have we not done many deeds in your name?" Then he will confess to them, "I have never known you, I know nothing of you" (Matthew 7:22, 23). On the other hand the most completely powerless, the absolutely lowest, sin-laden person who comes to grace, who has not one moment of time left to work and act for [the Savior], is in for just as friendly, loving, sweet [a] Lord and Master, as the one who has done works in God in huge number.

Now to be sure that is a dreadful thing for self-love to hear, that with all one's works a person merits nothing, that our best deeds, even if they were caused by God, are useless when we appear before his face, indeed [these works] come not one single time into our memory. For when the Lord will say to those on his right hand, "You have fed me, you have given me drink" (Matthew 25), they will know nothing about it. There remained with them no impression of it. Works follow along after us; therefore we do not even see them. The good that we do is not even worth a reward; because where is a single deed done for Jesus, which did not already have its reward in itself? That one may be allowed to serve him is already a reward of grace which is accompanied with so much delight and contentment that when it is done with, one is more ashamed that he was used than that it should be attributed to Jesus. "And if one would indeed anywhere cheer what belongs to the work of grace, then holy shame comes near, and shows us [in] all sorts of ways, that one thanks God, when one forgets oneself and thinks of nothing except that there is a Savior."[3] That is the way it is for the laborers of God, his true servants have it so good. It requires nothing but determination, [nothing] except faithfulness and sincerity. But if they want to merit something, they have nothing but difficulty and dismay. Because he gives the reward as he will. He gives the same to the last as he gives to the first (Matthew 20:14). If a person becomes one with the Savior only because of the reward, he will not curtail [the person's] rights, and will certainly perform what he promised; but [such a person] must not be discouraged if afterwards someone who merits nothing at all gets exactly the same. Whoever thinks to obtain honor, glory, or any other happiness with the Savior now or in the future, brings himself so much the more rest and peace than he had [with] secondary ideas; and if he comes away from it without greater misfortune, then he has God to thank.

It is a disgrace when a creature does not know how blessed it is to love Jesus, when she thinks that there is still some other blessedness which can be given to us in heaven that surpasses the Savior and his love, which would be more than when he said, "I am yours and you are mine." Since for this reason we are saved people, for this reason many heavenly people dwell in this veil of tears and so many of them know their Jesus; because eternal life depends upon appreciating this final message of the holy Trinity, which originates from their most high means (John 17:3). This is a truth concerning which I have reason to testify, without having to be ashamed before the Savior and some societies or without saying too much. It is truth. It is a truth of experience. I am brought by this means so happily through this world; whether I am at home or traveling, alone or in a group, whether I am comfortable or surrounded with extraordinary troubles; I could not allow it to occur to me, to depart from my Lord. Praise God that I am with him!

---

3. This is a hymn text. It calls to mind Luther's remark that those who are most concerned about their own salvation, hence themselves, are the most damned.

What the disciples said, "Where shall we go, you have the words of eternal life" (John 6), has not ceased to be true after his ascension. He is with us every day until the end of the world (Matthew 28). "Blessed are those who do not see but nevertheless believe" (John 20). He left behind for us in the Gospel, in the doctrine of his blood, an impression of his cross, of his death, of his merit, and of the salvation built upon it, so that whoever sees his Redeemer a single time on the cross, and catches sight in the Spirit [of] the form in which he was bled to death, has got something which no devil, no world, no glory, no suffering and no training from inside and outside can steal. "I am certain that neither death nor life, neither angels nor principalities, nor powers, neither what is present nor what is future, nor any other created thing is able to separate me from the love of God which is in Christ Jesus my Lord" (Romans 8:38–39). Therefore also the chief summary of all of this is what one can say in service or all circumstances, anyone individually or in the whole, "If only Jesus were your Lord! If you only knew even for one moment what manner of Lord he is, and would love him rightly!"

The world must promise much (I will not say whether the world keeps its promise), if it also keeps it and does more than what it promised; that is still not enough compared to the One who does not simply promise nothing, but rather promises suffering, burdens, humiliation, poverty, persecution, [and] death on account of his name. That is the salary [one is paid, and] at the same time one is so peaceful, so delighted, and has little thought about changing one's Lord and entering into the service of some other, as if one would be with some other lord and enjoy all the glory and wealth of the earth. Only those who have experienced this can believe it. It is a thing which is against all nature, which is even contrary to all other methods taught to us from infancy on, or which we can imagine, [so] that one cannot find oneself in it, one must have grace. Even the disciples of the Lord Jesus himself could not find themselves in it. Peter was described by the Savior as a man who was grounded upon the rock, but he said, "May it not befall you. No, it must not come to that." It is no renunciation, which is excused through reasoning, no inclination, which is imposed by argument. One can bring to that point, that he knows nothing more to answer; but when according to circumstances, when real arguments come, when tests come, then persuasion does not help, then one sees how little they [i.e., rational arguments] yield.

On the other hand, let the Savior lay hold of a soul only one time, let him allow only one glimpse into his reconciliation, let the eye only one single day turn to him conscientiously and be withdrawn from other things, so that [the soul] comes to know, feels and discerns, [the Savior's] blood, his death, his merit, his eternal, ardent love, of which the disciples spoke when he walked with them, when he talked with them, when he explained the Scriptures to them: "Did not our hearts burn?" After this, one needs nothing more; one is then his possession. I can also speak to this with great certainty. I heartily invite you all to give yourselves rightly into the contemplation of the suffering of Jesus, and to take time for yourselves to do it. I hold it to be worthy to postpone all other things until one is ready with this one, because I know and recall the delight, the tenderness, the inclination to him, the love which sprang up within me, when I heard for the first time in my life that Jesus died for me, [a condition] in which I still stand today and from that hour on could do nothing else except love him and proclaim his death as the most venerable, the most beautiful, the most love-worthy and blessed thing in the world. It is the thing which the most completely simple-minded person can grasp, a thing which even the most knowledgeable, the most completely wise, the smartest, the most well trained, the most honorable person must feel, believe, and experience in his heart like the smallest child. That here many sorts of things are left behind, that many truths can still be absent which the Holy Spirit would gladly [have us know] over and above that, and that still various things remain over which one would have to be ashamed in [the Savior's] presence when grace so abruptly and suddenly comes to pass, I do not deny; because love for, longing for and the inclination to [the Savior] goes faster than thoughts and reflections. Therefore Paul calls such people "untimely born" and says he would have been such in his own time.

But precisely in this we experience and see what a good Lord we have, how faithful he is, how tenderly he deals with us, how long he watches us, how he knows the way to make something good out of all our imperfections and our defectiveness, how to bring forward all the things held back, and how to compensate through his faithfulness and singular wisdom for what is lacking in experience, what is lacking in coherence, what is deficient in concept. "No more is demanded of a head of the household than that he be found faithful" (1 Corinthians 4:2). But we can take for granted that as long as we are spiritually dead, and do not have life, one can have no impression of his masterly skill in one's heart and the understanding cannot grasp it. No doubt one can get all sorts of things in one's head; in the depth of oneself I suppose one can ponder over many things, and experience a stirring in the heart. But the living, abiding impression of which I speak, which grows up with us and is no more to be separated from us, so inhabits us that he always goes with us wherever we go—where we eat, drink, or travel, there he is with us; he inserts himself under all discourses, in all circumstances, among all dealings and activities of life. This impression does not let us do whatever we want anymore, but rather binds us to the Savior's standard. But the same impression can never come until the person lives, until the Son of God allows one to hear his voice, until the blood of Christ takes away the dead essence and the stony is made easy to handle, as the prophet says: "I will take away the heart of stone, and give you a heart of flesh" (Ezekiel 36:26). That is the work of the blessed message of the blood of the Lamb, which in the blink of an eye melts the heart, and [before which] death must retreat, thereupon life gets a place.

If only people did not set their hearts like diamond, did not harden themselves against the strong prompting of the Savior, did not seek help in books, in people, in amusements, and in all places where they think they might find help, in the hour when the Lord comes with his Spirit to plant the word of the cross in them. That we do this many times our conscience tells us. How often have we noticed that the Savior was near to us? But how many times have we helped ourselves once again, so that his work is not able to reach its objective? What is more, in our times it has become a disgrace if one lets oneself be conquered by the Savior, and on the other hand [is considered] an honor if one can resist all the inclinations, the courtings, the truths of the Gospel.

One need expect nothing from one's conversion, except that one is hated, ridiculed, and persecuted by one's friends, by one's neighbor's, by all who have known one. That is true. It is difficult to follow the Savior within Christendom, and the person who wanted to escape the cross, made a journey over the ocean to the New World because he believed [he would] be more secure, more safe, among the wild people than among the Christians. But as soon as one knows from the heart that one belongs to the Savior, these things do not matter any more, but rather one remains a happy person. The heart rejoices and no one can steal the joy. "I will see you again, and your hearts will rejoice, and no one will take your joy from you."[4] This surrender in the hour and moment when the Savior calls has an influence in the whole life. One is then not subject to the hardships with which the poor souls have to drag themselves along who so often knock in vain.

Now I must still give a couple of words to how one has to conduct oneself with one's vocation, that one therefore not walk [in a way] inappropriate to it. Many have the idea: "If I wanted to be the possession of Jesus immediately, I could not do it, since I have [another] Lord, [another] Master; I have something else to do; I stand in [certain] situations with this person and that person." That is what for many people tends to be made a hindrance: But what connection has that with our Lord's service? One can hang on in all things in the world that are not sinful in and of themselves. What special convictions one has of one's condition, are different for another person; since what is harmful to one is not to another. A thing can be good for one person, while it is troublesome for another; something can stand under divine forbearance for one person, which God does not tolerate at all in another. But generally speaking there is no other measure in all outward situations, in all dispositions, in all actions—let them be commanded or stand permitted in holy Scripture; by doing these things the Savior can be called the Lord over them. Since all people in the world are his, all creatures are his servants. And what is more, even the servants who stood under the yoke of the pagans were supposed to carry on their lord's business, which often appeared strange enough, for the Savior. "You serve the Lord Christ," says the apostle (Ephesians 6:7). Therefore Luther also says: "If a maid sweeps out a room, she can do a work in God." "Whether you eat or drink, or whatever you do, do it for the honor of God" (1 Corinthians 10:13).

The Savior is so closely united with his servants and maids that he actually stands behind all their trifling matters. What they do with true joy, and to be sure not with the aim of lining their own pockets, [or] lead[ing] a comfortable life, [being] honored, [or] satisfy[ing] their passions, but rather on the basis of the truthful foundation: "It is my office, I am commanded, therefore I will do it from the heart"; this is the thing that he consecrates, that he reigns over, that he supports, that he defends: there he is in the midst of it as we see with Joseph in Egypt, who to be sure still lived through troubled and dark times.

---

4. This is another hymn text.

It is not necessary to martyr oneself in order to get certitude in [these] matters. The Savior demonstrates to his servants in the simplest way possible, in the most natural way possible, what does or does not please him. He convinces them also of what he does not want: But it is an unfaithful servant who, when his master moves, does not that instant abandon all happiness, all well being, all honor, all glory. Trials there are, but he does not impose them for an extended time, rather he is punctual and precise. As the Upholder of the whole world he wants that everything should happen in its order; and it pleases him when his children are scattered abroad here and there upon the earth and that his disciples sanctify all situations, all vocations, all businesses, as all those do whom the Spirit directs. Therefore, one might freely wish, and it would be very good, that the whole city and the whole country could be filled with servants and maids of Christ, moreover that they on that account neither altered nor abandoned their vocations nor their social stations, but rather simply got a different heart, a different spirit, a different driving force, a different motive, to impel their dealings and actions. That would be very delightful to the whole human species; even those would enjoy it who do not know Jesus, who stand under the forbearance of God and are not yet his children. Thus looks the service of our Lord that is grounded here: "Your sins are forgiven"; and at the same time begins: "I want to, be clean."

Those who not only confess Jesus, pride themselves on baptism, [and] participate in the Lord's Supper, but who also perform the smallest most unimportant action in order to bear witness that they belong to the community of God, but do not love the Lord Jesus have a special banishment placed upon them, they are cursed by the apostle; just as the ancient witnesses of Jesus enacted the ban in the presence of the members of the community, for example, Ananias and Sapphira. But whoever does not go along with the external matters of religion, who stands free [and says]: "I would rather not belong to the Savior"; who lies partly under the apprehension of the future wrath, partly under the universal corruption, in which one puts on the plague like a garment, and it does not let go of a person: all is death around one; all is accursed and the whole of life is only a curtain preparatory to the dragging away of all the corruption and misery and hell, and when the outward hut is broken, then one suddenly lies in a puddle without knowing any further how to save oneself. That is a wretched circumstance that to the people who are in it makes honor and riches, crown and scepter, all palaces, all glories and all happinesses of this world into desert wastes and completely places of horror. Concerning this, the experience is such that one can refer to oneself, since the experience lies in all people and conditions. But the experience of how good one has it with the Savior awaits the voice of the Son of God.

Faithful and Dear Savior! I ask you like a child, that you would take them up in your arms, those who up to now and in these days still are fallen, allow all those who have been permitting themselves to be pleased to hear the testimony of your sovereign authority, of your eternal peace, of your eternal love, of your eternal merit, and how good one has things with you, be near to them all, that you would attend to them all, let them all feel your glory, so that you can enter with your Spirit, so that you can forgive them their sins, take away all their death and corruption and receive them into your kingdom; and all their remaining life, all their circumstances you want to make completely peaceful and joyful; because you are the good Savior, to whom souls are so precious, to whom they are so important; [human souls] are your reward and your joy, they are the crown upon your head; accept all of them. The Father has entrusted them to you. You shall be their king and their leader, you shall dwell and travel with them. Do it, and begin, the sooner the better, especially among those who stand before you here, to exercise command of the heart, which passes over all understanding and organs of perception, and pour out peace, which is above all reason, for the sake of your faithfulness. Amen.

The Seventh Speech
(16 March 1738)

He Who Redeemed Me,
a Lost and Damned Person

"I HAVE COME TO KINDLE A FIRE UPON THE EARTH; AND WOULD THAT it was already burning!" (Luke 12:49). That was the Savior's passionate word when he came to the subject of the execution of the great transaction of our salvation. When we speak of the salvation of all of us, the nature of the thing brings us to three main considerations: First, that we are lost; second, that we are damned; third, that we shall be saved, or as it might be said much more radically and completely in our article: "that we are already delivered." These are the three things that we always have to keep in view, namely, that we are lost, damned and redeemed. And we are all three things at the same time.[1] That is to say, each person who neither has nor knows Jesus, who is in the presence of a servant of Jesus Christ who knows about the secret: [that each and every person is] a lost, damned, but also already redeemed person.

Therefore it comes about that the children of God do not easily get angry about evil; because right in the middle of all the wretchedness, right in the middle of the most irrational actions through which they

1. This is one of Count Zinzendorf's ways of expressing Luther's paradox that the Christian is at the same time justified and a sinner: *simul justus et peccator.* We always need grace and daily forgiveness. We are always beggars before God. We are always, even after we have been Christians for a long time, sinners in ourselves and righteous by virtue of a righteousness which is outside of us, which we have not performed but which has been accomplished on our behalf by Jesus. We wear the righteousness of Jesus Christ which God imputes to us. Our only righteousness, our only hope, is Jesus Christ himself. We must learn only to "creep into Christ." It is precisely over this point that Zinzendorf and John Wesley separated. Wesley could not accept this paradox.

hurt themselves most of all, one notices that they are rescued, and can be as we are. Because one knows what one is oneself, one is what one is through mercy. One knows that one is just as lost as they are, and not better than they are [though] redeemed through the blood of the covenant.

A person who has been pervaded with this truth can effortlessly avoid all other obstacles which offer resistance to the craving, the longing, and the love, since one would gladly speed souls along to the enjoyment of their redemption; because one would be happy to help them into the land of the living. O how one wishes that the sufficiency, the blood poured out for them all, the grace of Jesus, would be administered to them also one time thoroughly in the present, and would be manifest to their hearts and consciences so that it is evident before the tribunal of God, and they would therefore also have consolation in the enjoyment of it. But how does it come about that we least of all converse about our redemption, that we ourselves doubt concerning it when we take a look at ourselves, that all conversions begin with a doubt not only about whether we are saved, but rather [about] whether grace is able to come even to us? How does it come about that sorrow and anxiety are the first thoughts of a person who comes to him or her self, who awakens from the dead, hears the voice of the Son of God and begins to live?

This comes about because one first gives no proper thought [to the fact] that one is lost and damned. Because if we would believe that, we could more easily grasp and make sense of the other[2] as well. We are lost, says Isaiah. "All we like sheep have gone astray, everyone to their own way," (chapter 53). To be lost means, according to the general understanding: First, not to be where one belongs, and not to be able to be found by the people who have to seek us, [and] because of error not even to be able to find oneself. Second, it also means to be far away with no hope for any happiness, health, and life, that one has no likelihood of ever being able to attain health or life again. These two are meant when people in the world speak of "being lost."

Now, spiritually, it has this meaning: we have lost our map and way to salvation, we cannot find our way home again, we do not know where we are or what we want or require. Paul says, "In their ways are simply ruin and heartache, and they do not know the way of peace,"

2. The "other" referred to is our salvation, our redemption by the mysterious and powerful grace of God in Jesus Christ.

(Romans 3:16–27). It is almost unnecessary to get mixed up in an argument with people concerning [the fact] that their ways are nothing but disaster and grief. Since it simply is not long, [before] they sober up from the very drunkenness in which they suppose that things are good with them, and no one gently leaves the world who will not prove and seal with respect to their own person, "in my ways were nothing but catastrophe and sorrow: and my days have flown away and have experienced nothing good." As long as they go thus, and consider themselves no doubt with their sins, [but] not seeing their danger, they can also still make good progress so that it is not exactly unbearable to them, but rather it is quite easy and pleasant to transgress; one must have patience with them and not seek vainly to criticize them and hold them to be miserable. Because one accomplishes little when one talks about serious things with a drunken person.

Since they are also drunk, lost, dead, not knowing themselves and not knowing at all that they are on the erroneous path; people who would gladly say it to them and want to convince them of it they see as dangerous, or as people with whom it is not worth getting involved. Therefore, it would be a bitter and painful work to preach to the heart of a person who knows nothing of the self and does not think that he or she is lost. But something comes to us to help us, that is to say, the inward condemnation. "He has closed up all people under unbelief, so that he might have mercy on all" (Romans 11:32).

If people are often still so confident, and do not worry themselves about where it will end up; then the gracious hand of God comes over them and makes them tremble before his judgment and be terrified with fear of the great danger. They do not know where they should begin. They are persuaded that they cannot elude or evade him, but rather whether it takes a long time or short, they must come into his hands. Here they get an inclination, a punch, which they cannot easily resist. "His word is a hammer which smashes rock" (Jeremiah 23:29). And as God did in the Old Testament with the Law, so it happened many thousand times more with the Gospel in the New Testament. Because instead of as it was before when the Law knocked on the hearts with violence until it found a way through: so we now have the penetrating power of the blood of Christ, which flows and soaks through human hearts in such a way that their hardness is more softened by it than if they had stood in a glowing fire, that the most hardened hearts of all, the most obstructive, (who became as assured of their affairs as one can become of sin), come to know the potent hand, the mighty demonstration of the power of the wounded Redeemer and Lamb of God, of whom they can hitherto make no idea for themselves, their hearts have no feeling of it. This almighty strength of the blood and cross of Jesus is the first blessed effect, after which one notices that people are persuaded that their hearts are dead no more, that they are miserable, that they lack true life, that they are damned.

But a lost person, a dead person, who has no trouble, goes about in sin without knowing it. [Such a person] does not ponder even once the covenant of his or her baptism. We do not now want to investigate where it comes from [or] how it happens that the great power of the covenant of the sacraments, taught in our religion, learned by heart, [and] generally conceded, repeatedly makes no impression for so long, nor is taken into consideration, but rather the sacraments are forgotten like a dead person. But in the meantime [there] is no more controversy: there are hordes of people who fall out of baptismal grace, who can no longer rely on [the fact] that they are baptized, to whom that dying out again of baptismal grace happens. Since, they received grace there, they were washed with the blood of the Lamb; thus they not only sank into death again for the second time, but rather they also fell back into all the former filth. Therefore, it is necessary that such people get their understanding made clear, not through art and human wisdom, but rather through a clear voice of [the] divine Word, [they must realize] that they do not know themselves, that they are dead, that they have no spirit, as Jude says, that they are in the situation where the Spirit of God can make no advance with them, because they are flesh, (Genesis 6:3) as it was for the first people of the world; that [clarity] makes an agitation in the depths of their very selves, that makes them quite cautious for a few hours, but it has no duration, rather it changes. One often and many times finds circumstances in life, [such] that they repudiate and excuse everything again and ask people who think themselves wise for ways out to go into their former darkness again.

But if the voice of the Son of God comes to the heart even one time, if it commands: "You are lost and undone," and the person is permanently convinced that he or she is in this manner damned and wretched, afterwards the person is already not lost any more, but rather found. A soul which sincerely from the heart holds itself to be damned is already looked upon as a member of the family [of God's people], if it can say in truth: "I know I have no part in the kingdom of God, I am damned."

Such people are found souls, they are found by the true Shepherd who has taken all our sins upon himself, who leaves ninety nine behind in the wilderness and goes after the lost one until he finds it, he has grasped it with his hand and laid it upon his shoulders; only the comfort is still hidden before their very eyes. All that happens with such a soul who is bowed down under condemnation is [the] child's play of wisdom and grace; whoever sees souls in this manner, whoever rejoices and thinks: "O of course! The Lamb pays the ransom for the poor children who regard themselves as lost, as warped by and entwined in sin." According to the mind and will of the Savior, out of these circumstances one comes to nothing but the enjoyment of redemption.

The enjoyment of redemption consists in that one knows and can say with candidness of heart: "I, a lost person, am found. I, a damned person, have received grace." We do not make progress if we wish to prove this holy doctrine to people who have experienced nothing of it. Since one cannot form a further opinion, as long as the preceding sentences have not yet become clear. As long as it is not revealed to a soul that it is dead and lost, the preaching of grace is useless; the message of the Gospel accomplishes nothing. It may be that a person becomes pious, betters herself, does good things, is seen as good by everyone and has it said of her: "That is a changed person." But with the bloody grace there is nothing to be done until the person has recognized herself as damned. After that the Savior becomes the preacher to the poor, and all his servants are then such people. That is to say: "Grace streams from Jesus ' wounds, [so] that one can say 'Abba,' and one sees herself from that hour on as a child of grace."[3]

But then, in what does our redemption now consist? Obviously, we shall speak of it more properly and more fully if we catch it in the text concerning the precious blood of Christ: so it is nevertheless necessary to say a few words as a prelude to it.

Our redemption consists in the most absolutely astonishing truth in the world, which no clever person will hold as a "baby food" of reason, because it is a plain bit of silliness according to modern methods of reasoning, concerning which the apostle Paul candidly confessed: "I preach the crucified Christ, to Jews (that is, to those of my religion)

3. This is a hymn text.

a scandal, to Greeks (that is, to all other intelligent people) a bit of foolishness."

But then, in what does it consist? In this: The God of all the world, who is as truly the Son of God, that is, God by virtue of origin, as a human being is truly human, in the love of his Father, through the instigation of the Holy Spirit but from a free will, consented to be humiliated and to become a human being in the form of sinful flesh through physical birth for this reason, because sinners could be helped in no other way, to grow little by little like other babies, to be brought up by his parents, to stand in a submissive relation to them, to remain unnoticed into his thirtieth year, so that one hardly thought of his name, finally to stride forth to teach for a couple of years and after many wonders and endless demonstrations of his goodness and truth, with the gain of a few souls, without seeing his disciples one time in the situation that he desired for them, to die a shameful, terrifying, wretched, damned, according to the manner of that time, death before the gaze of the inhabitants of a great city, to hang on the cross as an evildoer to be spat upon, laughed at, [and] exposed to ridicule, between two wicked scoundrels who hung next to him and also slandered him; and of course [he agreed to this with both] the intention to redeem and with the consequence of redeeming the whole human race from all sin, of liberating the entire earth from the curse, of releasing all souls from the devil, from death, and from hell, and of propitiating the Eternal, the Original Righteousness, which was offended through our sins, of placing mercy over judgment, of obtaining a conquest of such a kind that the world never thinks nor will think, namely, in an instant, through the surrender of his spirit into the hands of his Father, and through the laying down of his body in the earth, of putting into action the best thoughts which the wisdom of God, the understanding, the will, the counsel and love of God decided upon: he rose after several days, in all peace [he] went down among a few souls to whom he made known the secret, taught and so to speak held private lessons with them, where they were fundamentally and accurately instructed concerning the kingdom of God so that they could be his witnesses in all the world, and after this accomplishment [he] was raised up over all the heavens, he sits omnipresently at the right hand of the Power as the Head of all his faithful, to rule the world, but in the form of a Crucified One,[4] in an image in which he and his faithful often appear

4. Zinzendorf literally says, "in the form of a cross." His point is that the rule of God

as if they were nothing, as if they were made only to suffer, and had to be a spectacle of the angels and the world. But the rest of the world, that is, almost all souls for whom he died, go under his eyes and patience, and do not see themselves much according to him, according to his redemption, according to his death and resurrection, as they would do if a little bird had gotten away by flying.

The truth of his bloody reconciliation is to be sure a divine truth which wins acceptance from us, the ones who believe, the ones who are filled with love, devotion, and awe, and in time and eternity can be guarded from all sins. But it is not everyone's thing to believe this. Amen! I bear witness before all who hear me: it is the greatest grace, after the incarnation and death of the Savior, the highest blessing, and the deepest miracle if God makes us believe in the name of his Son, that is, [causes us to believe] that Jesus Christ is God the Lord, that he has redeemed all souls with his blood and torment, done away with sin, endured the baptism for which he longed and which so terrified him before he completed it, and gained himself an authority as a human being to become the Preacher who speaks more mightily and with more healing and wholesome effectiveness than Abel and all witnesses; the Teacher in whose words are located human salvation, deliverance, and grace.

We shall preach this idea and no other, indeed any other word is a great misfortune. The apostle said, "I know nothing else." Paul, the wise, intelligent, learned, and experienced man, knew no better wisdom than Jesus Christ and him crucified, (1 Corinthians 2:2). But one must first wait patiently until we find faith. Second, one must not turn against it. There are few who believe it, and they do not find themselves in us who teach that, and if they should be allowed honestly to talk seriously with us they would laugh in our faces that we believe such unseen things, and in the meantime we let go of everything that is obvious and visible. Our comfort is that here and there a soul which because of the power of the blood of the covenant finds his way to the forgiveness of sins and, although under prostitution by the world, exclaims with us, "He was slaughtered, and has bought me with his own blood."

---

in the world, the way in which Jesus is the world's true king is radically unlike all earthly powers. Jesus rules precisely as the crucified and broken man. Not pomp and might but suffering love and self-surrendering mercy is Jesus' way of ruling. Not force but yielding, not crushing the sinner but allowing himself to be crushed in order to redeem and win the sinner. That is Jesus way of being the world's true king.

The Eighth Speech
(19 March 1738)

Purchased, Won

"ALL THINGS ARE YOURS, BUT YOU ARE CHRIST'S" (1 CORINTHIANS 3:22). "For this reason Christ died and rose and became living again, that he might be Lord over the living and the dead" (Romans 14:9). "They were yours, and you have given them to me" (John 17:6). These are three different places in Scripture which clearly prove and clarify the same matter, namely, that souls whom Jesus Christ has redeemed are great and mighty people who can, in all truth and without saying too much, claim that all things are theirs. Paul says, "The apostles are yours, all people in the world, let them deal with you or treat you as they will, all things in the world are yours, life and death are yours," what more can one desire?

If the enjoyment of this human privilege were permitted to people in their ruined form a great confusion and muddle would arise; because if they used all things as they use the few from time to time it would look very bad for the world; but that is taken care of, since all who still live in their natural circumstances are so little the "lords over all" that they are slaves of sin and death. But those to whom all things do belong are, through a secret of the world, unknown and stand under an obedience in relation to the true Redeemer, which the apostle names the "obedience of faith," an obedience which therefore comes, so that we know that he is our Lord, that we see him with our hearts as we might see him with our bodily eyes, that we hold to his cross and his death, to the redemption through him; thus we can love from the heart none other besides him.

The Israelites were cured from the bites of the fiery serpents by looking at the iron serpent; we look upon Jesus, the Author and Finisher of our faith. And so it happened during his lifetime to the sick and the oppressed, they looked at him with the eyes of faith [as] they wept under their affliction. With these eyes we take our hearts to him so that he and we enter into the most deeply inward and tender intercourse. In addition it happens that we take the yoke upon ourselves, the necklace, of which the Song of Songs sings: We go in bonds of love, and they [i.e., these bonds of obedience in love] are at the same time our jewelry on the garment of salvation and on the dress of righteousness. It is also called the badge which we wear as a pledge of his love and of our faithfulness, that we do not do what occurs to us, but rather that we are drawn through a gentle impulse to have no other mind and will than the one Mary had with all her bliss: "Behold, I am the handmaid of the Lord" (Luke 1:38). "I am your servant" says David, "You have destroyed my bonds" (Psalm 116: 16). When the old bonds are broken the new ones begin, so that "you now belong to another" (Romans 7:4). In other words: "He died and rose and lives again for this purpose, that he might be Lord of both the living and the dead." He came to inaugurate the kingdom of God, and now Christ is Lord, to the glory of the Father, and we are his subjects for three reasons: first, he redeemed us; second, he purchased us; third, he won us. These are three different titles or powers.[1] Redemption takes place through a price that is paid. The purchase [takes place] through difficulty and work. The victory or conquest [takes place] through battle.

In the first place, the Savior redeemed us. On the past Sunday I have explained that the whole world is redeemed. He gave himself, says the apostle, for the redemption of all (1 Timothy 2:6).[2] And that shall be preached until the day he appears again. Therefore, the Holy Spirit already says through Zachariah that to us it is given in consequence of a costly oath, to be "redeemed out of the hand of our enemies to serve him without fear our whole life long in holiness and righteousness,

1. "Power" here means something like a political office. It means he has the right and the authority to administer something. The Savior has the privilege and the authority to dispense justice and mercy.

2. The rejection of a limited atonement is classically Lutheran. Among Calvinists the view had developed that Jesus died only for the elect. But Lutheran theologians, Zinzendorf included, said, "No," pointing to New Testament passages like 1 John 2:2. Jesus Christ died for the sins of the whole world.

which is pleasing to him" (Luke 1:73–75). And in conformity with these words, the Savior himself says to his disciples: "Go into all the world and preach the Gospel to all creatures; whoever believes and is baptized will be saved; but whoever does not believe will be damned" (Mark 16:15, 16). Why? Because one does not believe on the name of the only begotten Son of God. Since God did not send the Son to judge the world, but rather that the world might be saved through him. Whoever believes in him will not be judged; but whoever does not believe is already judged because they do not believe. This kind of person could not accept it if one wanted to say they are already saved, since their hearts think quite otherwise.

Thus we see what stands in the way of the whole world, not only all the scoundrels and unbelievers in all the nations, all the savages, all those who are animal-like in their behavior, all the devourers of their fellow human beings, but also the respectable people; both all the distinguished people of rank and the humble, all the learned and all the lay people, all the professional servants of God [i.e., clergy] and all the scoffers and blasphemers, all the brutal people and all the virtuous, all the philosophers and all those of a foolish nature, in a word, all who are not saved, and why [are they not saved]? For no reason except unbelief. Since he was given over for them all.

According to Holy Scripture there is redemption from many things. He has redeemed us from the future wrath. He redeemed us from all unrighteousness. He redeemed us from the dominion of the devil, from the present evil world. But in a fatherly manner he also redeemed us from our vain and empty way of living, which is a completely different expression. In its scriptural sense "redemption" means an action where a thing or person who finds him or herself in a miserable condition is set at liberty in some way, the old owner can make no objection to it because he is, so to speak, reimbursed. The redemption of humanity takes place through a ransom. Since that is the formula in which Scripture expresses itself in so many places either explicitly or in such a way that to think of it is the unavoidable conclusion, it always serves.

One of the most important passages of Scripture which confirms this is when Peter warns the people not to imagine that they were bought with gold or silver; No, not with gold or silver, but rather with the precious blood of Christ, an innocent and spotless lamb (1 Peter 1:18). From this it is clear that a whole new religion was begun, and that one would have to sever infinitely the holy truths of the Lord, tear them asunder, insert and remove them, if one wanted to rip apart these holy and great words "ransom for sinners" and set forth a different meaning or image from the tone and basic idea of that word with which all salvation is brought to pass.

Straightforwardness and truth is doubly necessary with the use of Scripture, otherwise we prostitute our holy doctrine through the application we make of it. But it is also true that some twisters of Scripture mean no harm. Because they hold instead when they read the Holy Spirit's so astounding and, according to their way of thinking, unfitting forms of speech, they have to help him, they have to make something more sensible and more coherent than what is there, the holy text has not expressed itself rightly [so they think], something different must have been intended. I candidly confess, these same keepers of the word and of the divine wisdom present themselves to me as very worthy of compassion, and the weakness of their understanding is apparent. I believe in a naive and simple way what the nature of the words [of Scripture] carry with them, and I hope on the foundation that eternal wisdom will have known, what it has spoken and written better than all people, better than we know it, because we first must learn there.

If we assume that [plain and straightforward approach to Scripture], as it must be assumed, then this truth is perfectly clear, we have truly been purchased, we are paid for, just as a person buys a good thing from someone else; just as one buys the freedom of a prisoner, just so have we been ransomed from wrath, from judgment, from curse, from the Fall and all its corruption, from sin, death, the devil, and hell, by means of a true, effective and complete payment in God's currency, namely, by means of the blood of the One who by God's grace tasted death for us all.

Israel was redeemed in a righteous way, and its prisoners most justly (Isaiah 1:27). It was inevitable that they would be redeemed by an eternal righteousness, by an eternal redemption. Because they were handed over and sold through a pronouncement that was about as easy to revoke as the edicts of the king of Persia, of which it is said that they cannot be either changed or revoked. That is why even Ahasuerus[3] did not repeal his command against the Jews, but rather could only permit

3. Ahasuerus is the king in the book of Esther. Through her influence upon him Esther rescues her people from destruction.

its weakening, so that the Jews might defend themselves. The authority and power of sin and death stood fast in the deepest foundation of eternity. It was common knowledge before that court of justice, whose pronouncements in their unalterable limits and constitution are effective and in force through all eternity. But now it has taken this course: Satan, who really had souls in his fetters, prisoners to his will , (because to the one they had given themselves as slaves in obedience, they were slaves indeed) who is able to make no objection, that very Satan carried out the counsel of God.[4] He filled the heart of Judas, so that he betrayed Jesus. He induced the people to bring Jesus to the wood [of the cross], so that they killed the Prince of Life, so that they took upon themselves and their children the danger of his death and blood.[5] In any case, he must now relinquish them to the One they abused, the One they crucified, and who through this abuse and death inherited them all anew, to God, to whom belongs vengeance: "His vengeance appears, he will repay." Indeed, he will love all his enemies, bless those who curse him, do good to those who hate him, pray for those who abuse him:[6] because he is the only begotten Son of the Father he thinks that way. In a word, we are free from the devil.

4. Zinzendorf's claim belongs to the heart of Christian teaching. There is only one God and Lord, one power, who rules over all in eternal and sovereign majesty. Christianity is not dualistic. Satan is a creature, not an antigod. This mysterious and shadowy figure is not God's rival. It is instead just as dependent on God as are all other creatures. Even if Satan wishes to bring the counsels of God to nothing, it cannot. In fact, it must serve God's will and purpose. Therefore, whatever the devil does God makes to serve his will instead. The devil is, in Luther's phrase, always "God's devil." Though the Adversary may rage and tear, twist and pervert, in the end all its efforts will only redound to the praise of God's glorious grace.

5. The Count expresses Matthew's account of the sentencing of Jesus by Pontius Pilate. Only in Matthew's Gospel does the mob take upon themselves and their children the responsibility for the death of Jesus. One must be very careful here. This text, isolated from the rest of the Gospel testimony, has been made to function in the Christian tradition as a justification for the exclusion, persecution, and murder of Jews.

6. Zinzendorf interprets the Matthew text in light of Jesus' words in the Sermon on the Mount (Matthew 5–7). This is a radically different interpretation from the one which scapegoats Jews. Instead, it makes them special objects of his love and care! How many sermons, how many readers, have failed to understand this point, so dear to Zinzendorf? Howe many consciences and hearts have shuddered in terror and found no relief? The way of Jesus' life and his words tell us how Jesus is through all eternity. They reveal the true and eternal heart of God toward all people. Jesus is not an angry Avenger. Jesus is the humble Savior who loves us when we hate him, who seeks us when we flee him, who blesses us when we curse him.

The world, which sometimes binds us anew, to which we sold ourselves, because we are in a certain way free people who could arrange matters for themselves, [this very world] was routed along with Satan, their prince and god. The world, including us, was a slave of sin and death and could force no quarrel [with its master]. The world, too, stands under the one who can no longer hold his prisoners, but must let them go on account of the blood of the covenant: therefore, it can have no more claim as their master, as he who sends them. And therefore, we must also let the world go when a redemption is created. And on this basis the Savior can justly require that the very same people who are his be connected to their neighbors, including father and mother, not only if these [neighbors] belong to the world, but even insofar as they oppose or resist the divine call and claim on our hearts or gifts must freely say: "I do not know you, I know nothing about you" (Deuteronomy 33:9). Because they doubtless have an interest, the second and next interest in those who begot them and brought them up.[7]

But the Father who chooses us for life, who calls us to glory, who to that end gave his only begotten Son for us all, who perfected the Prince of our salvation through suffering, and finally has led out into [public view] the great shepherd of the sheep Jesus Christ through the blood of the eternal covenant, so that now all the sheep can come to him where he wills, he who has the original and first right to them. He is called, because it cannot be otherwise, "The true Father of all who are called children in heaven and on earth" (Ephesians 3:15).

Now we will examine the "purchase."[8] The scriptural expression is this: let the people who have been won [or acquired] come through. The New Testament explains this and further extends it: there the church is called the community of God that he won [or acquired] through his blood (Acts 20:28). The basis of this lies in the words: "Because his

---

7. For Zinzendorf, living by faith, intimacy with Jesus Christ, can never mean one severs ties with the world or with other people. It can never mean a retreat into a private sphere of holiness. It can never involve disassociating oneself from people who do not know Jesus, or who mock and scorn him. It means, rather, sustaining those relationships, loving those others, and living as a neighbor, in Jesus' terms, in relation to them.

8. The whole section that follows shows us Zinzendorf explicitly using the classical or *Christus Victor* model of the doctrine of the atonement for understanding the work of Jesus. This model is prominent in Zinzendorf, and produced the so-called blood and wounds theology.

soul labored, he will see the satisfaction of his delight" (Isaiah 53:11). It is generally known that the word "to purchase" is always used of the physical and spiritual pains, where one gains something either by hard and sweaty toil or by otherwise taking great pains. Jacob toiled 14 years for the sake of his Rachel, and six for the sake of his wages, after that he appealed to his father-in-law; "I am suffocated with the heat of the day, and tormented by the frost at night, and can get no sleep in my eyes" (Genesis 31:40). When we contemplate the life of our Savior, so worthy of glory, the long effort which he endured in the world, the thirty-year burden which he bore in peace and quietness, (but the little and unnoticed faithfulnesses are much better than those which attract attention), the last years of his teaching ministry, where he often did not even have enough peace and quiet to eat, where he toiled during the days and was sleepless during the nights, where he in the end acknowledged enduring such a labor of soul and spirit that bloody sweat was squeezed out of him; then we can believe that he purchased something for himself by it, why? Because his soul toiled. Therefore he is also called a servant: that is, a worker, a person who puts forth a great deal of effort.

Assuredly if we consider our Savior's labor, and behold how easily we move through the world, then we must be very much ashamed of ourselves. The people who properly concern themselves with their business expend much labor and effort in their fashion; but what is it really in comparison with the inhuman exertion of the Son of God? "Who in poverty and difficulty allowed himself to be trained on our behalf; Who had no peace at all; Who sweated blood with his severe effort."[9] Through this labor we are actually purchased in a special way as his reward, and (as it is expressed otherwise in the prophets) as the fulfillment of his delight (Isaiah 53:11). We find the words in Scripture from the Holy Spirit: "My delight is in humanity" (Proverbs 8:31). Thus the Savior takes his delight and joy in us, and he can even be fully refreshed in us, that is the reward for his infinite work. Do we want to begrudge him his joy? Do we not rather want to abandon a thousand joys in order to become the plaything of the Savior? Because otherwise one day we would have to submit with a thousand terrors and sorrows to the wrath of the Lamb, when he flares up; then we cannot escape, then we have to be blamed, and must lie and be thrashed under his stern and unrelenting scepter, if we have not wanted to kiss the scepter of peace. If we do not become his

9. These lines, taken from a hymn, rhyme in German.

pleasure, his joy and delight in this present awful world; if we dread his acknowledgment before poor, miserable people and do not confess here that we are his; then we must still in eternity lie at the footstool of his throne as adulterers, adulteresses and whores, who deserted their bride-groom without cause, and will cry out to the mountains and hills to conceal us from his countenance.[10] But in addition he has also won us. The emphasis in the foundation text is very important here, *thriambeuei hemas*,[11] "He leads us out as his triumph" (2 Corinthians 2:14). Since that is the natural application of the word in all places where it is otherwise to be found, it has the sense of "to drive out" "to vanquish" "to exhibit as a good consequence of his victory" as the conquerors of ancient times did, who had their enemies bound and dragged in front of their victory chariot as a sign of the courage, the glory and power of the war hero, king and prince. So it goes the same with us says the apostle: God leads us forth in triumph through the whole world and reveals through us the scent of his honor, the renown of his glory, and indeed in different ways; some people to their destruction, some people to their salvation, a scent for life or for death. "This one is set for the falling down and the rising up of people" (Luke 2:34). One of the ancient patriarchs says: "I won this with my sword and my bow" (Genesis 48:22). The Savior himself also helped him with his arm, so that the riches and blood of the enemy was splashed upon him (Isaiah 63:3). "He marched forth to do well for the truth, and to preserve the distressed with justice; His arrows were sharp, so that the enemies of the king fell there in heaps before him" (Psalm 45:4–5). For this reason it says of him: "He rides forth to victory and conquest" (Revelation 6:2). But it is not merely such a victory as [when] one drives enemies and rebels together, but rather [as when] one tears the allies from the jaws of the enemy and brings [them] to freedom; [they] afterwards go with him [their deliverer] as a sign of the honor and victory of their friend, of their protector and helper. "After your victory your people willingly offer sacrifice" (Psalm 110). Your enemies have to [receive this defeat] with terror and fear, but his people want it

10. Zinzendorf takes the fullness of the biblical witness seriously. He also always thinks eschatologically. The present is lived always in light of the future of Jesus. The Savior is also the judge. Judgment is real and will come in the end, but the Savior's people have been removed from it even now by faith. Zinzendorf proclaims the final triumph of the one God, and of God's righteousness.

11. Zinzendorf uses these Greek words, which I have transliterated. The Count's translation is in the next phrase.

with a thousand joys. The carts are his voluntary people, of which each and everyone testifies that he is a willing servant, a voluntary witness of the glory of Jesus. Thus Saul formerly had a city that was in the most extreme need to be delivered out of the hand of its enemies (1 Samuel 11). Just so the ancient servants of God always adopted their allies and delivered them. Abraham created peace for the kings among whom he lived, for which Melchizedek, the king of Salem, went to meet him and blessed him (Genesis 14). Our king Jesus acts in exactly the same way, Jesus, who was ours and we his, who was promised already in eternity, and [who] promised and pledged his body for the human race, (hence he is also named "the Lamb, who was slaughtered from the beginning") who truly earned us by his wearisome suffering in this world and finally on the trunk of the cross, under the image of a suffering person, the likeness of an evildoer, of a person who has been damned and cursed, over whom the sins of the whole world ran, [who] won the proceedings by the sweat of his face and fought the victory for us. He carried out the judgment unto victory, laid his enemies as a footstool under his feet and publicly displayed them; afterwards he went away in the very same spirit of victory, and preached it and made the doctrine of his victory generally known to those who would not believe, climbed to the place of the prison, captured and freed its prisoners through the blood of the covenant which still helps us every day and every hour. Because he has now truly redeemed, captured and won us from all sins; a special attention is called for on our side.

"How will we escape if we neglect such a salvation?" (Hebrews 2:3). It is preached, it has been made known to the world for so many years, it is still daily attested in such distinctive ways, it stands in the word of God, which is modest in all hands. Why have we not all long since [come] to have honor and joy in the pleasure of the very same redemption, the delight of the very same struggle and victory which Jesus attained for us all? He is so close then, to give us all things, he is so willing that we should have redemption through him, that each individual person should know, "I too am purchased, I am paid for, nothing else can make a claim on me." He would gladly like to make himself known to us in the very same arrangement, (from which no one can be excused) so that we are his purchased good, the bride for whom he worked, the friends for whom he fought, the reward of his cross, his plaything and crown, with which he was crowned on the day

of the joy of his heart, on that day which no one but he himself and
those who belong to him can call "joyful"; because the crown in which
he sees all his witnesses and souls as costly things braided into it, was a
crown of thorns here [in time]. As it is with the joy of his heart, so it is
also with his beauty: which is described in detail in the Song of Songs;
if one examines it according to those human ways of thinking, then a
very strange picture emerges.[12] But to hearts it is truly beautiful; the
torn, bled, hardened, benumbed limbs with which he hung there before
God and humanity and angels as a horror; was mocked, consumed and
mortally wounded, this is beauty in deed and truth which still daily
tears and wounds all poor sinful hearts, this is also the beauty to which
my heart is bound.

Because the martyr-form of the Redeemer who paid the penalty
for us was the natural consequence to him of our damnation, of the
wretchedness and vileness[13] of our souls: since he loved us unto death;
he declared himself publicly for us and toiled for us upon the cross so
that he might not hide us but rather might exhibit each one of us as a
trophy, as his redeemed covenant partners, as his people, whom he leads
through the world, to stand by them as a champion, and they [for their
part] fail to appreciate not a single day until the end of the world. "Today
you hear his voice, so do not harden your hearts" (Hebrews 3:15). That
means not so much that we will be compelled and constrained, but instead it merely means we shall not harden ourselves, which shows that
the advances are all made by him.[14]

The Savior does not need our help. He does not demand that we
prepare ourselves for his kingdom, he is wise enough, he is mighty
enough, he is near enough to open our hearts and to reveal himself to
us in the most fitting and appropriate way. On that we can depend. The
call of his servants goes no further than: "Do not harden your hearts because of this or that scornful honor, restless pleasure, dubious property,
[or] shameful laziness." If you feel assured, that is God's power, [just]

12. Zinzendorf's point seems to be that if one reads all the erotic imagery of the
Song of Songs in a natural "human" way, it seems strange. But if one reads it as language
about the Savior's love and about the intimacy of the Savior and his people, then it
begins to lose its strangeness.

13. This word also carries the sense of loathsomeness, frightfulness, beastliness,
hideousness, and the like.

14. The initiative always belongs to Jesus Christ and not to us. He comes to us. We
do not go to him.

do not resist it; do not permit the fantasy to dominate you that this or that person will despise you over it, ridicule you, forsake you, and make life difficult; do not allow yourselves to use this one or that one, things which you can either lose or acquire, do not allow yourselves to be beguiled and held back, or, even more importantly, to be pulled back into damnation again.

No person with a natural understanding, and who hears what is attested concerning Jesus, is able to approve of the matter and truth without thereby becoming enthralled. We Christians are after all not completely indifferent, if we only listen to the presentations about our Redeemer's death on the cross. It is a thing which lies in all the baptized, that they cannot hear that Jesus died for them without feeling. And if it happens again that way as it has come, we have no excuse as the Hottentots do [who can say]: "We have understood, felt, or been aware of none of this"; but instead a form of suppression [either] subtle or crude happens to one and all, and they can, when necessary, know how they each time get away from it again.

What then do the souls among us to whom the Savior came for life and peace, for grace and eternal redemption, know [how] to say? They know this, that he pursued them, not they him; that he took hold of them, not they him; that he chose them, and not they him. "He came for me" said David, "He desires me" (1 Samuel 22:17, 20). "I was taken hold of by him" testifies Paul (Philippians 3:12). "He reached out for me. I have been known" (1 Corinthians 13: 12). There is of course such a disposition, and people commonly already came to it through the seduction of worldly circumstances, that the natural sentiment and inclination of their hearts to what is not good far outweighs feeling for the cross of Jesus. In addition to this comes the evil practice of prattling on since childhood about the blood of Jesus Christ as about a fairy tale, which makes it so contemptuous over the passing years that one no longer knows what one should think and hold about it. To be sure all that cannot completely crush the feeling in the heart. But there is yet another universal corruption. Each age of humanity brings its particular special engagements, hindrances, and resistances with it; through which then the Savior with his redemption, purchase, and winning of souls little by little becomes, if not completely forgotten, nevertheless irksome or alien to the heart. It is astonishing that any people, when they just listen, notice it, and even if it is so plainly explained to them, still everything is a complete mystery. At the time when the truth still lay wrapped in images and parables and in dark sayings, which the danger of those days rendered necessary; when one thought people would not understand it, because it would be too obscure. From that time on one has spoken already a long time with circular words which are quite familiar, with such expressions that each one can grasp the meaning; one also speaks not without stirring people's feeling: but all for nothing.

Feeling itself is something questionable, so that if one cannot deny it immediately the very same minute, and something even remains behind I suppose, doubtless the actual influence of the truth is often over and done in less than half an hour, until something comes anew, which also strikes only a few minutes, and rushes away again in its turn. I do not know what I should have hopes of for my speeches. Since: 1) I have no time to perfect them, and 2) I desire to preach nothing great before you, but rather I strive after the whole matter, as an unformed and natural discourse in which I seek to speak with the frankness, plainness, but also profundity, which each upright person rooted in their station in life has observed in ordinary conversation. The simpler my presentation is, the more certainly it hits its target. Hence, follows the momentary conviction of the friends who hear me. But because presumably [in] the hours and days that follow from it, exactly the same method is observed which usually tends to follow upon the hearing of the word; as a result, presumably, with most people it will also have exactly the [same] consequences. Let it be to him as he wills it, thus it is said, heard, and I hope, attested in your hearts. You are all redeemed, purchased, [and] won together with one another through the merit, through the toil, and through the death of the eternal Son of God our Redeemer, our Head and Lord. Whoever now remains a slave of sin, whoever now dies under the tutelage of the old person of flesh, whoever becomes united with the enemies of the Lamb will want to scrape into the mountains and hills; after that the person will know, yes, will still more likely experience, that this was his will.

The Ninth Speech
(Undated)

Won from All Sin

"DEATH IS SWALLOWED UP IN VICTORY, O DEATH, WHERE IS YOUR sting? Hell, where is your triumph? Thanks be to God, who has given us the victory through our Lord Jesus Christ" (1 Corinthians 15:55, 57). It is an error [both] when we imagine sin as too strong and think there is no remedy against it; and when we conceive of it too frivolously and think it is still allowed. He wants to have mercy upon us, curb our misdeeds, and cast all our sins into the depths of the sea. And that is the victory that swallowed up death. That is the sea, yes the whole abyss of the mercy of God which is covered with the blood of the Son of God as the earth is covered with water. He sinks the banishment and the curse of all sin and never again allows it to rise. Like a sunken stone.

Death is the exact opposite of that to which the love and mercy of God in Christ Jesus helped us. God created us for life, which we lost; but whoever has the Son of God has life again. Whoever does not have the Son, the image of God, is still in death (1 John 5:12). The entire skill of humanity in sustaining its outward life consists in that [people] prevent the corruption that lies within from getting the upper hand. The servants and maids of God carry bodily death upon them just like others; nevertheless they hinder the corruption in them through the grace of the Savior, and through his blood their land grows green and blossoms. They are completely free from spiritual death.

The old ruin which is contrary to the meaning of Jesus, the horror-lake of original sin in which natural people[1] swim and, as the apostle

---

1. In other words, people who live apart from Christ.

said, "drift away on" (Hebrews 2:1), and [which] believers wade through as through an ocean of dread, and around whom the waves crash, is a true hell indeed. For the most part people think of sin as if it were a charming thing; in that case, how could it be called a "sting" or "thorn?" The Savior states better how it is with sin: "You are of your father, the devil, and you act according to your father's desire" (John 8:44). Each person who is subject to carnal pleasure, to avarice, to pride, and to comfort is a slave and at least a houseboy or housemaid of the devil. And if [such a person] obtains his or her imagined goal and acquires the honor, money, pleasures and comfort she has searched for; then she is and remains behind the cauldron, the court jester of the devil: outwardly [such a person] is respected by people according to characteristic human emotions, is considered to be worthy, prosperous, enviable, brought over, and so forth. But this happens only when all goes according to desire.

On the other hand, when people have been plagued and tormented for twenty, thirty, or forty years and not obtained what they sought, or lost it again after having had it; then they will be sought after and derided by all the world as fools, proclaimed to be supercilious buffoons, misers, wretched persons, and adventurers. That is, in the end, the reward for all their effort and work; and at times precisely from that time on so that one can half and half set his horoscope by it.[2]

The inner mercy of the Savior moved him to send his messengers to people, to open up their eyes so that they could turn from their darkness to the light, and from the dominion of Satan to God (Acts 26:18). If we then want to see good days, so we should allow ourselves to be returned to our good Lord. So that our sins are annihilated and the time of refreshing comes from his face (Acts 3:19, 20). The astounding thing is not so much that people commit a transgression once, but that they can put up with sin [as a continuing daily reality], because sin is such a miserable and intolerable thing. But this has a secret cause, and if one knows it, then it is easily comprehended. It is customary in the world that after people do hard work, they relax and refresh themselves. And that gives an opportunity to ask people who are often all too restrained and calm: Where must the powers come from? Accordingly, one tends to give people something to cheer up their nature, when things become

2. Zinzendorf means that the "reward" begins when a person's fortunes change for the worse and continue from that time on.

a little too much for them; and the sinner must also get that, otherwise they would simply let the work lie. If there were no law set forth in commandments the wicked heart would remain exactly as it is, but its eruptions would be much rarer. But because human nature is so constituted that when a thing is forbidden, which a person has neither seen nor desired, it gets [when it hears the command] first a special inclination toward the [forbidden] thing; it is good to comprehend what Paul says: "The power of sin is the law" (1 Corinthians 15:56). The Gospel now makes a mighty stroke in this. [The Gospel] cancels the character of the command, makes the soul free, turns it away from all rules toward the heart, toward the anointing, toward the feeling of grace from hour to hour as often as the occasion comes, toward the new or rather restored nature which one received from above after being released from the old guilt. With that troublesome sin loses its power and livelihood; the soul has no more desire for it and a lot is left lying.

Where does all this come from? Where does the weakening of sin come from? From where does the holy Gospel come to the other side? "Thanks be to the blood, that now flows through all things."[3] "Thanks be to God, who has given us the victory through our Lord Jesus Christ" (1 Corinthians 15:57) When he died he liberated us for [the purpose of] good. Even if we might have been fond of all sins, they are sunk in the ocean of the blood of Jesus Christ. All who hear this and believe it, and whose heart wants to become so, can still today have it and experience it. There is no sinner who is excepted here, no matter how he or she may be deceived by Satan and with what means or to what extent he will, no sinner was left unredeemed and unpurchased, there is no sinner to whom Satan has not lost his rightful claim.

Do you want to be saved, you fornicators and thieves, you wrathful persons and murderers, and liars, and, whoever you are, you dejected and unbelieving, who hear this word? (And who now read it?) Then know that Jesus paid the penalty for all of you, and that you could experience in this instant that you have been saved through his wounds (1 Peter 2:24). The fountain stands open, which is given against all sin and unrighteousness (Zachariah 13:1). "Accept absolution and look on him, and believe, and rise up and rejoice, and get dressed and run."[4] Therefore he died for all so that they, who now live, might henceforth

3. This is a hymn text.
4. This is another line from a hymn.

live not for themselves but rather for the One who died and who rose for them (2 Corinthians 5:15). We are his and belong to him. As we were formerly a plaything of Satan, so from now on we can be a plaything of the Savior. The very same things in his service of which the world says, "That is a burden, a cause of complaint," become to us a delight and a joy. "Whoever dies to the world, [and) eagerly asks for living faith, will soon palpably perceive that no one is destroyed who dies to the world."[5] We are his marriage partners, won with his own blood, the reward of his roughly thirty-year-long effort and work. We eat and drink, sleep and wake, work and rest for him. He fought for us [to win us] from the dominion of the devil: he presented the case against Satan. He entrusted us to his Father at that time conjointly as he said, "Father, into your hands I commend my spirit." With that God got us back again. "Your former selves have died, so that you could be another self" (Romans 7:4). That refers now to [the fact] that we live, as soon as we have grace, as we would have lived before the Fall, blameless, holy before him (Ephesians 1:4). Only more blessed and secure. Because he is now our Lord, we must also be his people, follow him and serve him. Whoever lives as he lives, must necessarily be hated by those who hated him and also loved thus. But whoever can say in addition, "I live, and now not I, but rather Christ lives in me" (Galatians 2:20); goes over all difficulties to the other side and [the difficulties] barely make an inner impression. Because she or he is redeemed from all sin.

---

5. Once more, this is a line from a hymn.

The Tenth Speech
(20 March 1738)

From Death and from the Dominion of the Devil

"JUST AS THE CHILDREN HAVE FLESH AND BLOOD, SO HE BECAME A partaker in the same, so that through death he might take away the power of the one who has the dominion of death, that is, the devil, and redeem those who through fear of death have to live as slaves throughout their whole lives" (Hebrews 2:14–15). One can be convinced instantly about the kind of Lord one has, if one has it explained from whom one gets one's salary or wages. Holy Scripture also demonstrates it in the same way (e.g., Romans 6:19). If someone has the gift of God for a wage, that is a sign that one is a servant of God. If someone has death for a payment it is a sign that the person is a servant of corruption, a slave of the one who can only give death, no matter what he promises, otherwise one can have nothing to do with him: Because he has nothing; the devil has nothing better in his capacity than death.

Death is not a dying in one's bed or in other circumstances, which a person is usually accustomed to call "death." We see that from the words of the Savior, who truly said nothing other than what was verified through experience, and in whose speeches lies the most experimental wisdom:[1] "Whoever believes in me will live, even if they die, and whoever lives and believes in me will never die" (John 11:25, 26). Hence it is very proper that we give a little thought to these words, because

---

1. "Experimental wisdom" refers to what one learns or can know as the fruit of one's own experience.

in these very words [is] the proof that that which people call "dying," or the laying aside of the outer bodily tent, is not rightly called dying, neither in itself nor in its consequences. Therefore Scripture too made a wise distinction between the first and the second death.

If human going out of the world were in and for itself a death; then it would remain precisely settled that the godless die once. But because the dear Savior knows, and his servants the apostles knew, that the death that follows this life belongs absolutely not to the actual connection of so called dying, they call it the second death. All things, all people who are born, belong under the first death, namely under the very thing which of course comes into the world through sin.

In what does this death consist? In that a person is born into the very same weakness, into the very same strength, into the very same circumstances as everyone else we see before our eyes; that is called having death at the neck. From the moment people are begotten they have death in them. The soul, which in itself can neither die nor change, which is from [conception] on imprisoned in a body of death and must go around in the world in that very body.[2] It must allow the motions, feelings and experiences which a soul, a free soul, could have, to be interrupted by another being, and sometimes be pressed in by means of a lead weight, to be unsettled through an accident, to be obstructed and have something in the way: that accordingly the whole natural life of humanity is a constant death. Therefore the Savior wants to say: "I cannot deny to my children and disciples that they die, they die everyday; but if they believe in me they can be assured, they will come into life, it will become better for them. If they live now and believe in me, then I stand in such a relation to them that they will die no more for all eternity." Now we can see completely clearly what the Savior wants to say. If the Savior had meant the natural going home, then he would have to have said that people who had Jesus would not go out of the world like other people. But why is it that when one had examples of people who

2. Problematically, Zinzendorf's way of speaking about the soul here is more Platonic than it is Christian or biblical. That is, he expresses an idea that draws significantly on Plato rather than on Scripture. It is Plato's view that the soul, an entity that inhabits the body, is higher and better than the material world. The body is said to be the "prison house of the soul." But that is not a biblical expression at all! The scriptural way of speaking is quite different, not least because the body and the material creation are not degraded. They participate in the salvation God works. God declares them good and very good in the book of Genesis.

went to heaven, now one has none since the time when the Savior went to heaven, at least none are known of? That is the reason the Savior cannot have meant, "My disciples shall not be decomposed," which is what people in the world mean by "dying," but rather he said: "They die from the moment of birth on, they carry the body of death on themselves, that is true. By dying and by experiencing every day that they have a fragile, transitory tent, with which their soul is encumbered, a body which impedes in all sorts of different ways; thus they shall consider and think about it, and be comforted by the following, "It will soon come [about] that we will live truly, so that death will completely cease in our members." Therefore Paul says: "It will be a good thing when I die, to die is my gain" (Philippians 1:21).

To call something "gain" means to get something better. How could it be that there is nothing better [than for] the soul to be freed from the tent, where would the gain be? There is accordingly a true gain in the so-called process of death. It is a refining of the blessed, who are made pure, [a separation] of the reconciled souls from their wretched huts, from a great encumbrance, which they carried in lowliness and patience, according to the command and order of God, according to the example of our Savior Jesus Christ, who also carried such a body and who did not say, "It is completed,"[3] before it was the hour when he was to be cut off from the body and delivered his soul into the Father's hands. Consequently, that is the beginning of life, as soon as the hut[4] is laid aside. After that there is no more dying. Then the soul gets no more such burdens hung around its neck anymore, but rather comes as it were into free air. That which formerly died, whose death we felt for such a long time and is now laid to one side, in the meantime is cured and placed into an incorruptible state through the miraculous power of God. Therefore, when we hear that our Savior rescued us from death, it means just this: He gave to his believers so that as soon as their outward journey ceases, as soon as the school days are over, as soon as they go through the days and years in the lowly frame, in which they must have to do with dying, according to the judgment and justice of the Fall; then shall they suddenly enter into life eternal, they shall suddenly be set free from their death, they shall stand there in a soul which has been anointed with the blood of Jesus Christ: as soon as the

3. The German word means both "completed" and "perfected."
4. The German word also means "tent."

shell of the hut, or the fragile, miserable, deathly, corrupt and perishable body is demolished, shattered and taken to pieces; then the soul shall nevertheless be dressed and not naked (2 Corinthians 5:3). Since they wear the righteousness of Jesus as a garment, if, as the apostle says in a completely German way, they have put on the Lord Jesus Christ in time (Galatians 3:27), and are found in that robe.

The other people collectively have nothing but horrors to await when the hour of departure comes. Why? Here to be sure they are just the same as the children of God, they have it no better outwardly; but inwardly they have a death which they do not feel, [which is] the most dangerous of all, a much more arduous death than the children of God. Why? Those who belong to Jesus crucify their flesh, together with its lusts and desires (Galatians 5:24), they know how to hold the body of death in discipline and order. They can hinder outbreaks of the poison of death a great deal through work, through faithfulness, through effort, through abstention, and so establish themselves that the memory, the feeling, and the reflections that they are dying fade away through their dealings with God and through their constantly being away [from bodily concerns] with their hearts in the presence of their treasure, which is of great value, through their work in the depths of their own selves and for other souls and the things of the Lord. "They do not reflect on this wretched life, because God brings joy to their hearts" (Ecclesiastes 5:20).[5] Therefore they also become less aware of the transitory hut than other people, because they cherish it less. So then the other people have nothing other to do than to feel their [own] death to be the most severe of all, because they are continually anxious and busy with the things which magnify sorrow and musing. Since if the poor worldly people who are without spirit go out of time they have nothing for which to hope: but rather when they are released from the wearisome hut, which is true and one has to admit it to them, and the soul is now free from the body; then begins the second death, then comes a new agony, then the soul is clothed again in something different, since it is naked. And this miserable and polluted coat has an effect that depresses the poor soul more severely by far than all the distress of the hut which one could still take off.

---

5. Zinzendorf's rendering of this text is a little different from most English translations of it. This may be due to his having quoted it from memory.

Here in the world one knew how to drive away the bitterness of death through all kinds of things and circumstances which Satan invented to falsify his servants' thoughts a little bit, to prevent useful sorrow, to hinder good reflection and everything which could make them reasonable outside of his fetters (2 Timothy 2:26). But when they are in eternity, then their past-times have an end; then all the same reasonings, all the same diversions with which one helped oneself in time [to overcome the bitterness of death] do not hold up any more, the ideas are demolished, the way to those good thoughts of oneself is impeded, those deductions are forgotten which answered those accusations in the heart by exonerating one: then the soul sinks into death; then it is judged, because it did not believe in the name of the only begotten Son of God (John 3:18). And that is a permanent distress, as soon as the soul in eternity, where there is nothing except truth, nothing more in false representations, but rather everything becomes visible in reality, falls into the second death with all its knowledge, beliefs, feeling and sensibility. Because now such an impending result, [even] if it is already manifested and charmed in a thousand fold way, always conducts such a careful punishment; souls will be held in slavery through it, and Satan does whatever he wants with them, because he has death in his hands, death with which we stand in such a precise connection, which belongs to us on account of our transgression, and with which Satan can drive into fear whenever he wants. He can corrupt for them their best days and most delightful hours so suddenly, that they do not even know where their own heads are. All this stands in his power. He is the prince of darkness, who does his work in the children of unbelief (Ephesians 2:2).

And as the servants and maids of Jesus Christ say: "He is our God, for whom we wait" (Isaiah 25:9), thus the poor souls who stand under corruption and under the tyranny of Satan, must know the very same [Jesus Christ] as Lord and Head, and must not stir against him, he is their God (2 Corinthians 4:4). It is generally known that free people naturally keep all things in much better order, if they are also equally subject. They also comply with their obligations, but that has its true measure, that has its purpose, if it is so difficult. They know very well: the house is mine, the field is mine, the land is mine; they have a desire to work on it and to do something. But if one comes into the lands where it is the ancient custom that people simply belong to their masters, who live in the same place and take half of the goods or lands that they possess, [and] are slaves in bondage; there one sees nothing but wretchedness and affliction, and in all the widespread estates nothing but poverty and hard times. They produce nothing. In good days they can scarcely support themselves, in bad days they have to die of hunger or become the last possible burden to their masters.

Where does this come from? They have no desire to do something; they have no mind to undertake something rightly. They have the idea, either true or false, deep within themselves through the inducement of external circumstances: With what thing shall I trouble myself, which can at all times be taken from me? This is exactly the way it goes for all the slaves of Satan, all natural people, all people who do not know where they should go with their souls even if they spend so much time on it, whether it is theirs or another's. In the same way, even when they hear [or] read the most completely beautiful things, have assurance of it; when they likewise think, "Yes, that would be good, it would be pretty:" when they want to catch hold of it, then they have no heart. Why? They are slaves through the fear of death and are so throughout their whole lives, through their whole [period of] being in the world. And therefore the beginning of all good must be made out of the grace of the Lord Jesus, out of his mercy, out of his reconciliation and deliverance from the dominion of Satan. Therefore he swore to deliver us out of the hand of our enemies, so that we could serve him without fear our whole life long, in holiness and righteousness, which is pleasing to him (Luke 1:74–75).

Naturally that brings me to speak about the struggle with sin. All people of upright disposition who read much, or otherwise have a good coherent understanding, are unanimous that one must not permit one's affections, one's sinful thoughts, enticements, inclinations, [and] cravings to have a free hand. There are irresponsible people, there are [also] wicked people, who do not acknowledge this. Each honorable person knows how to talk about self-control, and to recount how one restrained oneself in this or that matter in the world, how one controlled oneself in wrath, and broke the will there; how one would have been able to have this and that, but because one would have had to commit an unrighteous act, it was spoiled; how one here or there would have taken revenge, and could have made someone miserable, but [instead] had allowed reason and justice to have a place and [therefore] did not do it.

So it looks particularly with the disgraceful things, with the sensual sins and things like that. Thus one can construct for oneself little by little a whole system of virtue, especially of the virtues that bring us honor and reputation. The person, that is to say, who is otherwise so wrathful, is completely friendly; the person who otherwise holds so tightly onto what is theirs demonstrates a great generosity, this person has done much for each. Each person is otherwise extremely reckless and lascivious, but showed an unusual resolution in one or another matter; one has to be amazed, the person is otherwise so easygoing and does not gladly make enemies, but dared so much on this or that (simply as a matter of honor, simply out of a deeply upright disposition) that one is scarcely able to grasp it. Now in making a judgment one must nevertheless not be unfair. The world does not roll on quite as irresponsibly as people like to think; it also will require reflection; there were many quarrels deep in the self until finally virtue retained the upper hand and did what was right.

Now the apostle Paul tells of such a perpetual struggle in himself, when he was still a great philosopher and teacher among the Pharisees, when he assuredly grasped and understood all things which one must know and understand. He recounts extensively: When he wanted to do something good he was not able; he had an inclination to the good, but it was always soon thrown down into a heap again, something always took him prisoner again [so] that he had to do what he did not want, what he recognized as not right, what was not pleasing to him. Finally, things went so far that he no longer wanted to be a slave of the body of death: for he thanked God through Jesus Christ and drew the conclusion from his own example: "Christ delivered me from the law of death, he made me free from it; therefore, whoever is in Christ Jesus, whoever walks no more according to the flesh but rather according to the Spirit; there is no condemnation, neither over the former nor for future sins; for those who are in Christ Jesus the law of death no longer applies" (Romans 8:1–2).

As long as he reasoned, as long as he envisaged the commandments, the bounden duties, then it was impossible, the law always produced anger in him; it made him confused, and brought him into opposition to God. But what has God done? He sent his Son into the world in the form of sinful flesh, on account of sin, and condemned sin in the flesh (Romans 8:3). Paul discovered that when he was ready, when he was suddenly freed from the power of sin and death. Hence, as long as we do not have Jesus, as long as we are not personally engaged with him, as long as we have not found our salvation and deliverance in his blood, just so long we have to struggle with sin and we have to fight and martyr ourselves And that goes on after a person has a good, sincere disposition, after a person shows good, natural understanding, probably [it goes] so far that the person finally does not know what to do, and that there is more than one example of persons who actually became mad over their good intentions, for no other reason than that they wanted to become pious, they really wanted to do that , but were not able to do it. Whoever wanted to deny such examples would speak against experience. But whoever wanted to take advantage of this confession would only betray his lack of understanding. Since this is not to be denied; people who want to prevail over sin in their own battles and altercations by means of their own reason and understanding, by their own conviction and persuasion, who overthrew all danger, who are able to stop a powerless creature, are overthrown by one mightier. They are exposed to the fact that sin becomes Master, that in spite of all their battles and struggles the devil treads them underfoot; that it goes with them as David says: "The enemy pursues my soul and crushes my life down to the ground, he lays me in the darkness like those who are dead in the world" (Psalm 143:3). They do not attain to freedom because they become so exhausted and weary in the struggles and brawls and finally out of all forms of beliefs and sudden ideas fall into a reckless condition, in which one thinks little about God, but about the Savior not at all, therefore because all things one was promised by him failed to appear, because all the effort and work was in vain, and because people, if they wanted to compel and accomplish without him, nearly did so by their understanding and by all their powers, by health and life but it was no use. But all that occurred accordingly, precisely that they were servants of sin, they had no power to do this, they became criminals viewed according to the law of sin, when they wanted to reject a sin. They may be with none other than with their self-chosen Master and Husband. That is already so.

But whoever grasps the meaning in the perfect law of freedom and salvation knows personally that Jesus purchased us on the trunk of the cross with his voluntary blood and death, that he took away the power of death and brought life and everlasting being to light (2 Timothy 1:10), that sin can no more reign over us because we are no longer under the law but rather are under grace (Romans 6:14): such a person [who grasps the meaning] also understands the secret of how it happens that one becomes free from sin in a completely effortless manner, without protest, without lament and agony, and is so free from it that sin has to get out of the way and withdraw, or die, that Satan, who has sin in his hands and who needs people to behave according to his desires, himself does not dare to have to do with us any longer. One establishes as true either that [the devil] does not hurt us or disagrees with the devil [and says] that he finally must be transitory and fleeting.

How does this happen? One allows the Savior to give one everything, all the power of his victory and heroism; one allows the Redeemer to give one all his [i.e., the Redeemer's] righteousness, one confesses to him, "My Savior, I can do nothing, I am a laborer, I am a person who is burdened, I have exhausted myself, accept me, have mercy upon me, I can no longer draw breath, I cannot withstand sin, I cannot get the upper hand, rescue me from the body of this death, make me free from my corruption, grant me the motherly compassion of your heart, grant [that] your blood and death come to me to [work] good, say to my enemies: Be annihilated, cast my sins behind you, devour death in victory." Thus will the Savior soon take care of his people and concerns, "Whoever comes to me, I will not thrust out" (John 6:37). He well knows first that one can do nothing without him; one says nothing new to him.

When therefore such a wretched person who worked to exhaustion and accomplished nothing with it, comes to Jesus according to his word: then that is one of the first works which the Savior does in us, he sets us in forbearance, (as one is accustomed to speak of structures) he strides between us and the Adversary and says, "This child shall be unharmed."

Souls who now have gotten grace for the first time, who came out of death into life, who were for the first time begotten, who were found, when they were formerly concealed under the dominion of death, or who were dead according to the Spirit, whom the Savior now helped to life for the first time, [the Savior] first allowed to take a rest and to sleep, and afterwards he began to give them to eat and to drink. He nourishes them with his flesh and blood, cares for and tends them, and wants now gladly to bring them up, [so] that something shall become of them, that they grow, that they receive a character, and shall acquire a proper stature. Of this it is said: "Desire the reasonable pure milk, as newborn children, so that you grow through it" (1 Peter 2:2).

In time Satan must let us go, in time we are like a child in the cradle whose people are around to look after it. The child lies in a perfect peace, thus, [in] the first love, which the Revelation of John calls the most excellent and most perfect. [This first love] is with beginners so burning, so free, so full of life, that the good souls not without reason imagine [that] it could scarcely go further, one could have it no better in the world. It is true one couldn't possibly have peace from all enemies more than in the highest completeness of the age of Christ. Therefore it is a foolish, thoughtless speech and a sign of the utmost inexperience, when it is said: "People have not yet come far, they are only beginners; therefore they do this or that sin, therefore they have this and that wrong in them." A beginner is the best, a beginner in the kingdom of Christ who got grace for the first time, who receives forgiveness, whom the Savior has barely just taken upon his shoulders to carry home with joy, who is in such security, which no person is obliged to conceive, who is hidden from all danger, who can say with David: "You lift me up out of the gates of death" (Psalm 9:13). Thus he says of his disciples when he went out of the world: "Whom you gave me, whom I have kept" (John 17:12). "My sheep hear my voice and I know them, and they follow me; and I give them eternal life and they will never perish, and no one will take them out of my hand" (John 10:27–28).

If people are astonished that the disciples had such well-being: Let the people go, he says, the Bridegroom is with them, the time will come when the Bridegroom will be taken from them, then they will fast, then they will mourn; but it will also become good again, their sadness will be turned into joy (John 16:20), and after that they will not ever stop again.

To be sure times come again, hours come again, when we have advanced, when we have grown, when we have enough power, when we feel strong, yes, strong in faith, and are attired with the armor of God, when the shoulders can carry something; thereafter the Enemy is given permission to sample what kind of people the children of God are, what the Lord has caused us to become out of our sinning, for which purpose God helped us: But then one keeps company with the devil in a completely different way than before. This is indisputable: One struggles with him. One gets out of the way of the world, one flees before it, and then one is best of all against it. But one holds one's position when Satan approaches us, and overpowers him through the mighty strength of God and through joyousness of spirit. And the Lord shortly tramples Satan under our feet. Sin is the most wretched, most miserable thing, a disgrace, a matter that is not worth thinking about, and if something of the old things crops up, if it wants to stir something up and make itself felt, then it must be killed in the most contemptuous way, just as vermin usually are. Active sin has neither right nor power. It is to be drawn even in the smallest way into no consideration. "Flee from sin, as from a snake, since if it comes too near to you it will strike you" (Sirach 21:2). In the New Testament the same thing is said in this way, "Do not allow sin to rule in your mortal bones" (Romans 6:12). "Whoever belongs to Christ should crucify [sin]" (Galatians 5:24). One must not grant sin anything; that it may do something, or put something into action. Its cohesion is destroyed because the Savior has shattered and demolished its fortress. He ruined its structure. We are able to see again, that a fighter[6] of Jesus Christ has only to be watchful, that their many smokescreens cannot pull themselves together again, but rather must always remain separate. Then a thought can once again come rushing in, then the seed that Satan has sewn through his cunning or insolence can once again show something of itself; but one walks upon it. One does not cast one's eyes in that direction, one does not even deign to give sin a glance. The faith that a child of God has, but especially the faith of one of Jesus Christ's fighters,[7] which is so active, when it is permitted to notice sin from a long way off, when such occasions arise or in such cases, or when sin otherwise insinuates itself: [faith] instantly has the anointing ready to hand and warns us; and this recollection of the Spirit is so persistent and powerful, that before sin can even pull itself together and strike an attitude, a believer has already completed sin's ruin.

Therefore John had it right both times. Once when he said, "So if we say we have no sin, we lead ourselves astray and the truth is not in

---

6. Zinzendorf uses the term *Streiter* to refer to followers of Jesus. A *Streiter* is a "fighter," a "battler," a "champion," a "combatant" and so forth. Disciples are those who fight the evil one with the weapons of the Spirit, namely, the Word and prayer. For Christians the real enemy is never another human being. People do not need to be fought against. One must fight the world, the flesh, and the devil.

7. The Count seems to make a distinction between different kinds of Christians. He defines in the passage what he means by the faith of Jesus' fighters.

us" (1 John 1:8). Because sin remains in us right into the grave,* it is in our flesh. But [he is] also [right] when he cries out, "Whoever commits sin is of the devil; because whoever sins has neither seen nor known him. The one who is born of God does not sin; his seed abides in such a one; such a person cannot sin, because she is born of God" (1 John 3:6, 8, 9). Then where does such a great power of opposition against such a mighty enemy come from? From [the fact] that God rescued us from the governing authority of darkness, and transferred us into the kingdom of his beloved Son, in whom we have redemption through his blood, namely the forgiveness of sins (Colossians 1:13–14). This was a little something said about death and the power of the devil, and because of our power, which we have as soon as we live [in Christ], as soon as death has given way, as soon as we do nothing in our present human life except hope, do nothing except wait with all the faithful for the revelation of Jesus. This is called the shelter among all the distresses of death: Nevertheless! A time will even come, when my death will die. Now I am dead, I died, I have been crucified with Christ; but I know an hour will come when people will think I am gone, I shall simply be buried, [and] they will think now our friend is done for, he has had it, now he has died; but I will think very differently in my soul, I will look forward to the resurrection. This is certain, I will return no more to the broken heap of this tabernacle. In this deathly form we will not see each other again, my body and I; my head will never again give me pain.

But is that death or life? That is to be sure a blessed condition; to be once over there, through with so many difficulties, through with so many misfortunes, through with so many hardships and so many troubling and dreary ideas, within which the world is enclosed. No earthly god, who is under the power of Satan, can look without envy at the most

---

* [Zinzendorf added this note to the published version of the speeches.] The reader is cautioned that at the time I gave these speeches I was still very much preoccupied with the high nobility of the soul and did not know how deeply infected humanity is with the Fall and with original sin. I learned to think differently about the matter since then and wish that each one might have grace to receive his or her soul back made pure, then the souls along with the physical members will not have half so much misery. [[Translator's note: This is an interesting note. It reveals Zinzendorf's willingness to criticize his own statements. He says that at the time he gave the speeches he did not understand some things as well as he might have. It also reveals a shift in his understanding of the human person and of sin. The rejection of his earlier view of the "nobility" of the soul reflects his deepening understanding of Luther and of Scripture.]]

humble, the most wretched and most miserable pauper, who serves Jesus. Because [such a servant of Jesus] necessarily has a princely spirit, a heroic spirit, that gladly gives goods and blood for the sake of Jesus, because he knows that he can become as blessed as his Lord. Certainly, just as a person was a slave throughout life because of the fear of death, so also one is a noble through the hope of life.

It is no wonder that a person would gladly have us back and for that reason put us to all sorts of tests. But it is impossible for us to be talked into returning to them. Nothing is so great or more important to us, than that it could still be possible for us to allow sin to make headway in the depths of the selves that we possess, against the life that is in us, and therefore we must stretch ourselves out day and night, because we know that we shall be transfigured into his image (2 Corinthians 3:18), that the very same One who raised Jesus from the dead will also make alive our dying bodies, our earthly tabernacles, for the sake of this: that his Spirit dwells in us (Romans 8:11).

The Eleventh Speech
(30 March 1738)

Untitled

WHOEVER CONFESSES THAT JESUS IS THE SON OF GOD (ACCORDING TO excellence) abides in God and God in that person (1 John 4:15). Thus things go on with a soul that has faith and life. As soon as one believes and confesses that Jesus is God from God, everything else follows from that: one becomes a child of God, one is willing to go into all things. After your victory your people will willingly make offerings to you in holy finery (Psalm 110:3). It is fair to number among the failings of the first Christians that they now and then let show a considerable hatred for the remaining people who were not Christians. And to be sure for those who were not Christians, it was not simply a question of [their having] evil wills, but rather the truth that Jesus is the Son of God was a thing that contradicted everyone, both Jews and Romans. Therefore, without an unusual divine light, people could not get there or believe it.

Today it is worse, it costs more to love people who dare to say that Jesus is the Son of God and in spite of that live in the most extreme recklessness, and only take part in what belongs to external religion, but aside from [the externals] actually drift into doubt, or betray unbelief in their mode of life. But the circumstances of the case are peculiar and we must have patience. The apprehension that formerly made it necessary for people to deny that Jesus is the Son of God now makes it necessary to confess it. As a matter of fact whoever does not believe that Jesus came in the flesh we want to leave behind to their Judge. Flesh and blood cannot reveal it to us (Matthew 16:17). Education, human convictions, and first principles do not inscribe upon the heart, but instead

94

the highest it can do is inscribe it in the head. It must happen through the light of which Paul said, "God, who called light to shine forth out of the darkness, has given a bright light to our hearts, that through us might emerge the illumination of the knowledge of the clarity of God in the face of Jesus Christ" (2 Corinthians 4:6). To the natural person it is foolishness and such a person perceives nothing of it (1 Corinthians 2:14). The disciples in Emmaus did not understand it, but their hearts burned (Luke 24:32). Fire must enter into the heart through the grace of the Savior, which fire he could not scatter about until he was baptized with the baptism over which he was so terrified, until it had passed away (Luke 12:49–50).

But now the divine fire is communicated to each individual soul if they do not harden their hearts like diamonds, but rather remain open. But who does that? Who keeps one's heart open if the Lord himself has closed it? Jesus still said to Thomas, when Thomas already actually saw Jesus' nail holes and touched his [wounded] side, "Be not unbelieving." Therefore it must be possible even then to doubt, even when one sees. "Faith is not everyone's thing" (2 Thessalonians 3:2).

But how do those look who truly believe through grace that Jesus died for them? Peter says, "Do not give yourselves up, as you did formerly when you lived in ignorance according to your lusts; but rather according to the One who called you, and he is holy, so you also be holy in all your ways. Because it is written: "You shall be holy, because I am holy" (1 Peter 1:14–16). Two things surpass our conception: the importance of the matter as well as that one cannot find words enough; and what one should make of the idea that one receives the divine truths if one applauds them.

A severe judgment would follow if someone once had believed and afterwards disparaged the covenant of grace again and wanted to pay scant attention to the blood of reconciliation. Each one must confess, if it is true that God became a man; then there is nothing that can relieve the burdensome responsibility to any degree except ignorance or the miserable unhappiness of unbelief: ignorance, if one has still heard nothing of [the Gospel]; unbelief, if one can not accept it, if the heart still thinks otherwise [than the Gospel]. Concerning ignorance it says, "God overlooked the time of ignorance" (Acts 17:30). While unbelief is the opposite of active faith, in other words an alien work in us that deceives our minds; in this way it still has something of the first race:

but as soon as the accent may be rightly laid upon our own faith, then the Savior's saying is clear, "Whoever does not believe is already judged" (John 3:18). Whoever feels in the self no damnation, whoever still lacks a restless heart, makes oneself that way through all sorts of wicked deeds; I do not pass judgment on these people: because [they] are probably not yet drawn; moreover [they] have nothing lasting in [themselves], if understanding and feeling already have also now and then in addition been so forcefully snatched to that end.

The Savior must always make the beginning. One must first hear the voice of God that wakes a person up, and if we remain awake, then we learn faith. Whoever never feels the wrath of God is dead. But if such a person is a baptized Christian, then she died another time. From the hour that a soul lives, that so to speak a Spirit from God comes over it, from that hour on the soul hears the voice of the Son of God that speaks of nothing except the blood of reconciliation. Whoever has life, and has heard the voice of the Son of God, if she does not know Jesus as her Lord, feels that she is lost.

But whoever believes, throws everything away and does not confer with flesh and blood, but rather inquires constantly into her heart, can be torn out of corruption in an instant and become a child of God, as soon as she flings herself down as a sinner before the Friend of sinners. He loved us and washed us from sin with his blood (Revelation 1:5). The desire of the heart, of the believing heart, that drove the sinner to the cross of Jesus makes all the difference. Then one needs not long to take account of the passions, inclinations and cravings, one does not need to better the self. It almost belongs to effort, when one has experienced the blood of Jesus that one again falls into the old sins.

Whoever has once rightly experienced Jesus, gives the Savior his heart, and then nothing pleases him more than the Savior and his disciples. There are two kingdoms, [the kingdom] of nature and [the kingdom] of grace. The former has its own system with which the Savior does not meddle. What he finds there he leaves and his disciples do the same. But to the kingdom of grace the most miserable begging scoundrel can have no more difficult an entrance than the prince and the highest person can have no easier an entrance than the lowest. It must be sought in the dust, in humility and in bowing in the presence of the Savior. "You needy children of grace, who have the bestowal of the sinners in front of many others and you have your good king to whom to be sure no mite is too small, endowed with nothing that is yours."[1]

All people are one before him. [They are] either souls saved through his blood or [they are] lost. All have sinned, all become righteous by his grace. They must become like brute beasts before him (Psalm 73:21), and stoop under his feet, until he himself pulls them out of these wretched circumstances. Grace submerges our sins, they become covered with the blood of the Lamb, just as the bottom of the sea is covered with water. But all that is for stable persons clear *petitiones principii* [petition of principle]. It is a doctrine of faith and not of the head that proves itself attractive through a divine flame in the heart. Because true conversion is an inexpressible, unbounded, and even to the witnesses themselves, astonishing grace. John wept much that no one could be found who was worthy to open the book and to read it nor even to look in it. Then someone answered him: "Do not cry! See, the lion from the tribe of Judah has conquered, the root of David, to open the book and to break the seven seals" (Revelation 5:3–5). It is not given to all to understand the word that Jesus came in the flesh, but rather only convinced souls and souls pervaded by the truth. These [souls pervaded by truth] also know the way of human nature, especially the great light-mindedness in hearing the divine word. They have great compassion with those [who do not believe] and do not know how they should help the people who wail and are in pain. The heart comes across in a movement. But they know that Jesus has come, so that all people can see into the book and there read their own names. There are indeed examples of such people who were light-minded about the Gospel, yes, who reviled it, and the Lamb even still had a triumph.[2]

---

1. This hymn quotation expresses the notion that the children are worthy only of ferocious judgment. But what they receive instead is grace, mercy, and forgiveness, to which they contribute exactly nothing.

2. This, of course, means there are cases where someone reviled the Word of the cross, rejected Jesus most crudely, yet came at last to passionate faith in Jesus Christ. Exhibit A would be the Apostle Paul.

The Twelfth Speech
(2 April 1738)

Not with Gold or Silver, but with His Holy, Precious Blood, and with His Innocent Suffering and Dying

"THEREFORE, SINCE HIS SOUL TOILED, HE SHALL SEE HIS DESIRE AND be satisfied" (Isaiah 53:11). This saying refers to Jesus' recompense for his work. The matter naturally divides itself, if we want to talk about the wage or recompense for Jesus' work, so that we speak about his work and about his payment.

1) The work is called a work of the soul. That which the Savior suffered in his body is not actually the thing through which we were acquired as his own possession. With his body he became a sacrifice for us upon the wood of the cross, when he reconciled us with God through his death, and quieted the fire of wrath. Those who go by reason in the matter and want to remedy the misuse of the doctrine of the cross and give satisfaction say: "The Savior through his death only wanted to make us pious and godly and into fine Christian people, and through his suffering revealed the way to holiness." But the true cause of the sufferings in his body was the redemption of humanity from the slavery of sin and the devil, and that he might make a binding and meritorious atonement for us on the cross, as the Bohemian Brethren sang.

We do not begin by becoming pious and holy, if we want to become partakers of the death and cross of Jesus, we become righteous through his merit, as sinners, without adding any work; if we only are able to trust him. But there must not be a phantom faith in our heads. Whoever can believe the reconciliation of Jesus while having served the

Savior in precisely no way at all, but rather much more has spent his days with sins, is saved, even if he entered into eternity in the instant he came to faith. That is the effect of the merit of the death of Jesus. But the point that is connected with our responsibility is that his soul toiled. He awaited his death for thirty and more years and knew that he would die for the sake of human sin. During the whole time he experienced everything that a human being can undergo in one's soul, all of our weaknesses, sicknesses, temptations and practices. This was all pulled together when he sweated blood on the Mount of Olives, when he cried from the cross: "My God! My God! Why have you forsaken me?"

During his life his Spirit was often very much oppressed and he wept many times: these sorrows acquired our souls for him that we might be his bride, just as Jacob had to win his wife through his long 14 years of labor for his cousin Laban. The Savior had to get by very simply and poorly in his human hut, and submitted to everything, including even death. That happened in a completely different way than with his witnesses. They are made a gift of the greatest joy for their suffering, but for him his tranquility and his joy were often disturbed.

2) The recompense for Jesus' labor is ordained by his Father. Two things were promised to him: He shall see his desire; He shall be satisfied.

1. He shall see his desire.

When we look at the present condition of the world we see how little the Savior is thought of, and when it even happens at all it is without sensitivity.[1] His children, few in number, are looked upon as nothing other than strange beasts in the world. They long for nothing but to become the recompense for the labor of his soul. That is their united ambition, their one ardent desire, absolutely their only craving. And to be sure they are looked upon as dangerous, dubious, and even thoroughly bad people, as those with whom one should consider not getting involved. If out of recklessness one allows them to pass for children of God, then that is the reason people remain as they formerly were, without emulating them.

---

1. Zinzendorf means that even when people do think of the Savior, they do so with a sense of indifference. They are unmoved. Hearts are untouched and unaffected. The deepest levels of the self remain cold. Therefore, engagement with the Savior is superficial at best.

People often fancy they have the capacity to be great if they only permit the souls of the Savior to be his own possession, to live for him and to proclaim their loyalty to him in the very midst of Christendom. What concerns the Savior? He desires humble things and gladly makes do with little. He has chosen only lowly things for his playthings. The ecstasy is great for a person whom the Savior identifies in his heart as one whom he desires. A human being can scarcely ask for more happiness. The Savior sees his desire in all those souls he knows are deeply affected by him during the period of their lives.

The desire of the Savior is sought [by him] more conscientiously and timely than ours. We sometimes have good hope of souls and can linger over them a long time, when the Savior sees in advance that it is nothing. His joy is therefore more moderate, he sees further and what we take to be charming, sincere and pretty much complete, he in his wisdom often sees as wretched and lamentable and less than half. But he also has more desire than all of us do, since he sees beforehand both what each individual soul can still become and everything that he will do then ten, twenty or thirty years in the future with those who are saved.

2. He shall be satisfied.

That is something so large that our understanding is not sufficient. To be satisfied means to get much of what one needs; to have as much nourishment as one requires, as much to eat as one has hunger. If the Son of God shall be satisfied, and his hunger for souls shall be satiated, then that must be something inexpressible. Then certainly more must take place than we can think or hope.

That in turn makes his fighters desire to work. The number of his souls must still swell into great myriads. Through this hope the fortitude and daring of his witnesses expands and their loyalty is stirred up unceasingly to go after souls. Assuredly the content of this expression goes so far that I cannot find words to express myself about it. He, who out of hunger and thirst ran after souls for thirty years and ventured even more in his death than the heroes of David to quiet the thirst of their prince: He who thirsted right up to the moment of his death, he shall drink and be satisfied. For us, who shall be the Savior's wage, it must go so far as that we can say truthfully, "I may have no honor, no possessions, no right or privilege, and no longing in the world. I happily have no more will of my own. His will is my will."

It is not enough to count good works on one's fingers. It is all his from the moment when the Savior reminded us and claimed his wage and we believed that he merits what body and soul can do as recompense. Therefore, it is a key point of which the servants of Christ must take note. When souls are dead and have not yet heard the voice of the Son of God, then one can preach to them too early that they are the recompense of the Savior. The labor's recompense is claimed for the Savior when he brings us the forgiveness of sin.

We first have to know that the Savior has earned us. That is the labor that the Holy Spirit intends sometimes by means of law with those learned and smart people, when he drives them into a corner and shows them how destitute they are, when he takes away from them all glory and all their imagined virtue, and convinces them that they are sinners. That causes first that they learn to think highly of the merit of Jesus, and when the Savior forgives their sins, then the doctor falls at the Savior's feet and recognizes that it would be an outrageous and atrocious sin if he denied the worker his wage and Christ's bloody sweat of fear should be [thereby rendered] in vain upon earth.

The simple are nearer, because faith in the great suffering of their Creator and Savior for their sins tears their hearts into pieces and reduces them to a river of tears. "O woe that we have sinned thus!" "How fierce our sins, to arouse the gentle God, [who] can see thus out of affliction."[2]

2. These lines are from two different hymns.

The Thirteenth Speech
(Good Friday, 4 April 1738)

So That I Might Be His Own
and Live under Him in His
Kingdom and Serve Him

"LORD, REMEMBER ME, WHEN YOU COME INTO YOUR KINGDOM" (LUKE 23:42). These words constitute one of the most beautiful circumstances in the suffering of the Savior and illustrate the true idea of simplicity. He understood the sense exactly and answered, "Truly, I tell you, today you will be with me in Paradise" (Luke 23:43). The person who wanted to be inscribed in the Savior's memory was a thief, who was still unconverted on the cross, and not only did not regard Jesus as his equal, but even mocked him; since there were not more than two crucified with Jesus, they mocked him (Mark 15:32). It would be impossible for this heartfelt word not to have power, "Father, forgive them, they do not know what they do"* (Luke 23:34). The heart of one was awakened, or (as it is said of Lydia), 'The Lord opens up the heart" (Acts 16:14). And without scruple and without deliberation [that thief] simply said, "Lord, remember me when you come into your kingdom!"

The Lord, who wanted then to show us the method to save people, said just as simply, "Truly, I tell you, today you will be with me in Paradise." On account of this word the thief became as pure as an angel and immediately a companion of the Savior.

---

* Two public speeches were held concerning these words [of Jesus from the cross], but on account of the great crowd of people they could not be transcribed. [Zinzendorf added this note to the published speeches.]

That gives many people occasion for thought, as if nothing were necessary for entrance into the kingdom of the Savior except a good thought at the end of life. And it looks as if it were so. Because the example is nothing extraordinary, as many good willed teachers like to maintain to prevent damage, that something like that happens only every one hundred years, or indeed precisely only at the time of the suffering of the Savior. That is part of the process with conversion, and it is still happening to this day, if all circumstances concur. To be sure, more will be said about this soon.

We want now to speak about the kingdom of Jesus and of his subjects.

A. *The kingdom of Jesus is threefold.*

    I. The kingdom that he had before the foundation of the world, and continues into all eternity.

   II. The kingdom that he began by his future [entrance] into flesh and carried on until his exaltation.

  III. The kingdom that was initiated in part with his ascension, although under diverse *oeconomies*,[1] and continues into all eternity.

I. Before the foundation of the world he was truly the Son of God. He had the kingdom before the world was. For that reason he could say in his final prayer, "Father, glorify me with you yourself with the clarity that I had with you before the world was" (John 17:5). All things were made through him. "In the beginning was the Word, and the Word was with God, and the Word was God" (John 1:1ff.). He had the kingdom that endured in a majesty, honor and glory, from a source that we cannot imagine. One cannot say, "His kingdom began, *erat, ubi non erat*," [it was, where it was not] but rather it endured immovably and unchangeably, until he was pleased to pour himself out (Philippians 2:7), and as the children have flesh and blood in like manner to participate in the same (Hebrews 2:14).

II. Then began a second *oeconomie*, a new kingdom that had for so long been awaited. This kingdom is called the kingdom of the cross. The cross is nothing other than the image of the king as he looked, thus also

---

1. That is, the diverse forms God's kingly rule has taken within the history of salvation. Though the forms may be diverse, each is an expression of the will and grace of the same king.

the members of his kingdom appear. As yonder in Persia a king wanted to honor Mordechai highly and asked, "What shall one do to the man whom the king gladly wants to honor?" thus the honor consisted in that he was dressed in the official vestments and raiment of the king and was shown around within the city in them (Esther 6:6–9).

Whoever wants to be a servant of the Savior must share the condition of his Lord, share his shame and his cross. The whole kingdom of Jesus, if it is the most magnificent, is only glorious to souls who have a spiritual mind and taste. The Savior said that one should not say, "There [the kingdom] is." But one can very easily say, "There it is not." One can say, "No," without reflection to the description that the world gives of [the Savior's kingdom], the world that takes it to be glorious and great and constructs a nature of the true church out of its worldly authority and pomp. The Christians who are respected before the world do not prove by [the way they appear before the world] that they are people whom the king honors. They do not have his adornment, the nature of his princes, his splendor and pomp. Nothing in this kingdom can be found except undefiled delight, pure blissful hours, unalloyed rapture, but all within the heart. "The kingdom of God is righteousness, peace and joy in the Holy Spirit" (Romans 14:17), but for all who do not understand the secret [it is a] poor, wretched and contemptible kingdom, over which people think of a way to ascend as over a low fence. "The natural person perceives nothing of the Spirit of God, it is foolishness to such a person, and such a one cannot recognize God's Spirit, because it has to be a matter of spiritual judgment" (1 Corinthians 2:14).

III. The third kingdom begins to some extent with Jesus' glorious ascension and continues from eternity to eternity, but it will first become correct and right when those who still sweat in the kingdom of the cross are also brought in. His servants will serve him and see his face (Revelation 22:3–4).

What we can say about this kingdom is pictures, good concepts, representations and fancies. [But the reality] is altogether more than we could imagine and conceive; yes it is greater and more glorious than we would make it if we could similarly plan the best world in detail.[2]

2. This is probably a reference to the philosopher Leibniz, who had argued that the infinitely good God would create, indeed, had created, the best of all possible worlds. Zinzendorf asserts that whatever human beings might imagine as the best of all possible worlds is far less glorious than God's actual eschatological kingdom.

We are certainly saved. "We know not yet what we shall be, but we know that when he appears that we shall be like him, because we shall see him as he is" (1 John 3:2). The thief went into this kingdom.

B. *The subjects of the Savior are human souls.*

In terms of kingdom authority nobody is excepted, all souls are his (Ezekiel 18:4). "Now God chose us in Christ before the foundation of the world was laid" (Ephesians 1:4). "All our days that are still to be are written in his book" (Psalm 139:16). Therefore, we get the expression, "Cast upon God from the mother's womb on, to be appointed to a function or an office." He has us all already before him, and rejoices over each one's blessed share. That is the reminder of which Malachi speaks (Malachi 3:6), the book that John saw (Revelation 21:27), and of which Paul writes to the Philippians (Philippians 4:3), that the witnesses stand within it.

If we do not want to be his free and saved souls, then we would have to be his slaves. We must leave the body when he wills, that is all up to him. We must help to promote his kingdom, even if we have no heart for it. We must do everything in his kingdom that he requires, except that it helps us not at all if it does not happen from the heart.

He gladly makes all that is human and that is called human to be his subjects in the kingdom of the cross. "If I am lifted up from the earth, I will draw all people to myself" (John 12:32). He will leave no single soul undrawn. They are all appointed to be subjects of his kingdom.

People are appointed to the kingdom of the cross in three ways; in view of the time, in view of the things that they shall do, and in view of the things that the Savior wants to undertake with them.

The time in which a person shall come into the kingdom stands in the hands of God and lies hidden in the secret repository of his treasury of wisdom. If an eighty year old dying person, who was dead throughout all the days of his life and experienced and noticed nothing of the Savior and his kingdom in his heart, [if he] in the last hour of his life is drawn by the Savior for the first time, he is just as saved as that thief, and travels by the mouth off to heaven. Whomever the Savior calls in the final hour, with that person the Savior is also pleased in that final hour. Servants of Jesus Christ can count on this: that such [last minute] people are just as saved as they themselves are.

But that only holds true in the case of dead people, to whom it is a completely new matter** that Jesus Christ therefore died for them, that they do not live for themselves but rather for the One who died for them and who rose again. [In this way many thousands are saved, because confusion and bewilderment are so great in the world that it is impossible for many people in many places to find the right way and to be able to experience the divine truths with certainty. The thief represents a great multitude who in the end as poor wretched creatures, as inferior beasts, learn for the first time who Jesus is to them and what they should be to him. One does not first have to demonstrate a great reckoning of sins to such a poor human being, but instead refer him directly to the Savior.

The Lamb pays the price of redemption for such a miserable child that considers itself lost, that cringes and writhes in sin; if only it is true that the people formerly understood nothing, were not awakened, therefore also have not suppressed the fact and stirring of grace [within themselves].

Awakened people who have already known what Jesus and his cause is, who at their deaths can do nothing else except take a taste of accursedness, if one has not received Jesus or has turned away from him in one's heart. Whoever knows outwardly how she can be helped and does not accept it, either thinks irresponsibly about her sickness or suspiciously and distrustfully about the One who could help her.

And so go all souls with the Savior. If such souls could only conceive in the meantime a way and a heart for the Savior, in that way they would be helped. But it is quite a different story with them, than [it is] with the dead. It is a thousand times more difficult [with these "awakened" souls].[3] And the messengers of peace must target their utterance

---

** In the English language such a thing is called [being] "not guilty of religion." There is a great import in the word. They are not to blame that religion is the way it is, they have simply found it that way. [Zinzendorf added this note to the published edition of the speeches.]

---

3. There is a consistent theme in Zinzendorf that the conventionally religious, the upright. the publicly and externally moral, who are aware of and somewhat comfortable with talk about God and the Gospel, who know the catechism, attend church, and the like are the most difficult to draw into an actual, living relationship with the Savior. In the Count's view, such people tend to take refuge in their own piety, their own good works, or even in the objective truth of the doctrine, while their hearts, and the details of their lives, are far from and have little to do with Jesus.

toward this idea. Both types of people mentioned above now have nothing further to observe other than to accept grace.

But whoever is called early, when he still has it in his hand and time to make a move for the Savior, then that is a different story, not in view of pardon; because a four year old is saved in the [same] manner as an eighty year old, namely as a poverty stricken sinner: one has just as little right to be saved as the other. But in view of the future conduct, it is completely different; because as long as there is still time the Savior gives grace, and with grace power, to make a move in his kingdom and to bear witness concerning him. Whoever of this type of person only goes straight to grace alone, entrusts himself to it, and desires and does nothing more of that to which the Savior appoints him, such a person would deceive himself. Whoever is cleansed, the Father will wash even more so that he brings his fruit (John 15:2). From the hour on when souls have grace, they are in the service of the Savior; they may now be led and directed or only permitted, as it sometimes appears outwardly; but they are nevertheless led and directed by a good Spirit in their hearts. As soon as one has time for oneself, one must testify concerning grace, serve the cross, and live as a triumph of the Lamb.

In view of the things that the Savior gives people to do in his kingdom, they are very different, but they are in particular of two types. There are people whom the Savior uses in the ordinary way, and they are allowed to occupy themselves with those things that are so necessary to plain life as a citizen. They are able to do all that they do for him and to be actual, believing, and pardoned Christians. But there are also people whom [the Savior] appoints to his service in a special manner. They are called "disciples."[4] In the Old Testament we have the example in the pattern where each tribe had its own place and its own land, but the priests, who served the Lord in a special way, had no inheritance [of land]. Whoever is an authentic disciple of Jesus, has by all means something special within, not in bearing, not in behavior, not in dress or words, etc., but in the most important point.

---

4. Zinzendorf makes a distinction that the New Testament also makes. There is a great difference between people who admire Jesus and who have faith from a distance, as it were, and people who leave home and family to go with Jesus. These people who cast away financial and personal security, who leave their own whims and desires and ambitions by the roadside, and follow Jesus in his way of life, these are disciples. Their whole life and all their concerns are Jesus' cause, Jesus' Word, Jesus' Way.

In the fifth and sixth chapters of Matthew we find lessons that can be directed at no other people except at the immediate disciples of Jesus: for example, "If someone takes something from you, do not ask for it back again," etc. If one wanted to extend this to all Christians, that would cause all dependencies and all proprieties in the world to cease. A child of God, who hasn't especially dedicated herself to things of the soul, must submit herself just like everyone else in good order to the laws that everyone should accept as laws. In the Old Testament it is said to the captive Jews in Babylon, "Yield your necks to the yoke of the king, and serve him and his people" (Jeremiah 27:12). "Seek the best for the city to which I have let you be led away and pray for it to the Lord" (Jeremiah 29:7). If Christians on the whole wanted, especially in present day Christendom, to bypass the laws and to feign and bring about externally a prevailing indolence, then everything would go higgledy-piggledy and the result would be that nothing of the Savior's cause would be advanced.[5]

But with special disciples of the Lord it is completely different. That is a calling that has its own standard. One must not require anyone to become such a disciple, but rather much more hold people back. The disciples are always outlawed[6] in some place or other. There will never be a general sanction through which they are set free from the way of the cross, from persecution, from restriction. As regards the inner composure of the deepest self all Christians come to an agreement. There [within the self] one must make as little of honor as of wealth or of possessions, etc.; [disciples] must be both patient and unattached to

---

5. Zinzendorf's view was that the Sermon on the Mount was not to be applied to national or collective life. Moreover, it would not serve the purposes of God, he maintains, if Christians neglected the laws of the land in which they live. Christians should obey the governing authority and pray for the people and the land in which the Lord has placed them. His own missionaries were often charged with neglecting the law of the land. In this remark he is fending off these attacks.

6. In a very interesting move, Zinzendorf asserts, on the heels of his statement that Christians must obey the law of the land, that disciples of Jesus live "outlawed." He uses a German word that means "free as a bird." He is saying alongside his contention that Christians must obey the law, that disciples are not bound by any human regulation or control. Disciples live in a kind of freedom that is not possible to and does not exist for nondisciples. He is reflecting in his own way Luther's insistence that the Christian is simultaneously the free lord of all subject to none and the servant of all subject to all. See Luther's *Von der Freiheit eines Christenmenschen* (*Treatise on Christian Liberty*) in *Studienausgabe*, vol. 1.

earthly things. But in the external demonstration they are very much distinguished [from each other]. A fighter must every hour and at all times throw away all his right and claim and renounce all possessions and whatever else can be named, not only in the heart, but rather give all of it completely away, because another person can still demand his things and own them in peace.

To be sure it is a vast subject that we don't want to finish talking about today. We now want to see what the Savior has in mind with us all in his kingdom and what we have from him. The Savior now requires varied methods: He leads one through reason; to another the Savior sends many feelings in the depth of the self; to a third he gives a more systematic coherence as regards the word of God. Each person has gifts by nature that the Savior sanctifies when one has in his own way first laid it down in the dust and lost it for the sake of the Savior. We ourselves do not choose the ways, but rather the Savior does so according to our condition. Whoever has understanding the Savior will lead by means of it, and must only watch over himself on account of reason and superfluous doubtfulness and super-cleverness. But whoever has a tender heart the Savior leads through sensitivity and lively impressions of his grace and love. These enjoy their salvation in a more noticeable way, but must protect themselves against fantasies and excesses. The third group of people, who are theoretically and systematically ingenious, hold solely to the word, [and] renew their deepest selves so diligently that [the language of the Savior's kingdom] becomes to them eventually their natural language, they can be led very well by means of it, only they must protect themselves from deep brooding and speculation, more often than not from dry precision and inflated knowledge.

All is well, if one requires his justice. He reveals himself to people by means of a different way according to their best nature, and if they only need justice, when the Savior grants it to them they are saved by it in the world. All our good works are nothing but sheer salvation and grace for us. Therefore, one should not first wonder, "Why does the Savior demand service from us?" People think, "Whoever serves the Savior is saved. Whoever does not serve him is lost." The Savior alone devised our good works and demonstration of service simply by his grace and mercy, out of his love filled condescension to us. What if I ran? Well, go run! To work the works of God is grace for a soul (John 6:28). To be saved is its nature, and not, as ethics teachers suppose, an encumbrance or burden against which idea the prophet Jeremiah so fiercely campaigned in chapters 23 and 24. True holiness, which is from a humble heart, from a poverty stricken heart, comes from restored nature. Peter calls it the godly nature (2 Peter 1:4). Whoever has grace can be holy thus and it would seem outrageous to him to be otherwise. But the operation of holiness is distinguished from deeds.[7] One can be present without the other as we see in 1 Corinthians 13. Both can also be present together; but it is always in such a condition that it helps absolutely nothing with God.

Before God we are aware of ourselves, of our poverty, of our wretchedness, of our slavery to Satan and our service of sin. This [awareness] carries us to the Savior and says, "Because I am so destitute, so miserable, so defeated and damned, you have to help me." The work is continued in the kingdom of glory. There it will be perfect rest and joy for us both inwardly and outwardly; now it is still accompanied by many burdens and, it is true, even the humiliations of sin. When his servants see [the Savior's] face, then they will serve him. [Though] to be sure even in eternity our work is without merit. There is only a single merit to which we are referred both here and there; we are directed to the One who was slaughtered, and who loved us and washed us from our sins in his own blood (Revelation 1:5).

---

7. This point was very important in the argument Zinzendorf had with John Wesley. In the Lutheran understanding, justification and sanctification are one and the same. In the moment one is justified by God's grace in Jesus Christ God declares one to be holy. One's holiness, one's sanctification, is apart from one's deeds. Sanctification is not a separate process that happens after one has been justified and has begun to live by faith. So, for Lutherans, including Zinzendorf, language about grace and justification and language about holiness and sanctification, are two ways of talking about the same thing. John Wesley did not think dialectically and could not accept this classical Lutheran approach. For Wesley, holiness is observable, is about our works, and is a thing that grows throughout the Christian's life. Zinzendorf vehemently rejected any such understanding.

The Fourteenth Speech
(6 April 1738)

In Eternal Righteousness, Innocence, and Blessedness

"PUT ON THE NEW PERSON, THAT IS CREATED BY GOD, IN THOROUGH righteousness and holiness" (Ephesians 4:24). First we want to talk about eternal righteousness, innocence and happiness together, second about the method by which we can come to each one of them in particular.[1]

The means by which to acquire eternal righteousness is justification. Sanctification brings about our eternal innocence and redemption brings our eternal happiness. The thing that makes us so blissful in the kingdom of Jesus is called righteousness, innocence and happiness. We have to separate them according to time and see first how they were prior to the Fall, second, what their condition is after the Fall, and third, how they appear after the restoration and reconciliation of the Savior.

Satan disguises himself as an angel of light and sets against the divine truths things that should prove that he is that and also almost come out that way, but are even deeper errors.[2] According to this plan he has invented a different righteousness, a different innocence, and

---

1. For Zinzendorf holiness and happiness go together and constitute the same thing. To be godly and righteous is to be happy. That happiness that is proper to human beings and human life is what comes to one in and through Jesus Christ.

2. That is to say, the devil opposes to God's truth things that look and feel like truth, but are for all that even worse and more destructive errors. They are worse than ordinary errors because they masquerade as God's teaching while actually drawing one away from God. Thus, truth is subverted not through obvious falsehood and vileness, but through subtle lies that appear to be the truth itself.

a different happiness. They are distinguished from those of the divine standing in that they are not true and not enduring.

First, prior to the Fall we generally looked like this: we had wisdom, righteousness, innocence and happiness. They were true but as became clear in the way things worked out; they were not necessarily eternal. In particular we had a wisdom that I cannot describe, because I do not find it put into words in Scripture and because I do not wish to deal with thoughts and probabilities. True righteousness was that God created human persons for a purpose that he himself explains in Genesis 1:26–28, [namely] that humanity should govern and should make the earth subject. And in [that] state of affairs humanity could justly claim what belongs to us; because that is required for righteousness.

The Lord stood as the only person not under humanity and had prescribed a rule to humanity in which humanity should bind itself to witness that Jehovah is a higher throne (Genesis 41:40). In other respects humanity had the whole world under it; and the image of the invisible God was seen in it, [the invisible God] who gave to humanity an incontestable authority over all creatures in general and an indisputable power to each one in particular. Humanity could call in the fruitfulness of the earth and the splendor of heaven as a tribute that belonged to it. And it is not any more natural and innocent for an animal in the forest to take its food where it finds it, than it was to people in the original condition to use and to employ everything that was around and nearby.

The holiness of humanity before the Fall was based on the innocence that was unknown to them, what we call sin today, and [humanity] for that reason could not once concentrate a single thought on it. That is why humanity fell at the beginning through enchantment. Because Adam's feminine helper has the written evidence that she allowed herself to be enchanted and lost her simple intention. Sin certainly for the first time took its cause from the command, as it still always does.[3]

Happiness before the Fall was that things were always good for humanity, even work did not burden humanity. Humanity was knocked

3. Zinzendorf's notion is that the first human persons had an innocence of which they were innocent. They were unaware of their innocence because they were untouched by sin. There was nothing over against this innocence. There was no law to unmask any absence of innocence. This innocence was simple and natural. But it was lost through an enchanting promise of being godlike. It was lost through the effects of letting it go, thinking that in letting it go there would be delight.

around by nothing. Human rest and peace were not disturbed. The first humans had no concept of willing and not willing and their disposition was in such a condition that all by itself it would not have been possible to fall into the emotional disturbance that we call concupiscence, and which therefore becomes sinfulness for us because it is disorderly.[4] How would it occur to the first human to be something in this world? He simply was everything. How should it occur to him to desire something? He had everything. About what could he be anxious? He took everything he wanted. How could he become lustful? He was in constant pleasure. How could he become slothful? He could not grow weary.

Second, after the Fall it is completely different. Our wisdom flees away so that a person by nature, driven by concupiscence, longs to know everything that does not really matter and does not come to know those matters on which everything hangs. The cause to which we are destined we don't learn with pleasure, but rather preferably another, in particular in the business of happiness. Therefore, our wisdom is described as foolishness before God. It consists only in useless speculation and our insights are soon overthrown by others. What we know are things we do not need and are either completely unlikely or highly dubious.

Righteousness after the Fall consists in that we pull ourselves together, whereby we think to endure before God. I speak of such people who are troubled about God and who seek him, about the others [who are indifferent and do not seek God] one cannot also say that. The former seek God through all sorts and forms of public worship and through good works done for their friends, which soon slipped its way in among the Israelites, and still continues. Human righteousness for people who are concerned about God consists generally in that they stop doing wickedness and do something good instead, give alms, etc., that should help them. At the lectern[5] several contradict this. In practice they are almost all one.

Our righteousness after the Fall consists either in a dubious incomprehension or in a self-made holiness. Incomprehension is distantly similar enough to innocence before the Fall that one still neither knows

---

4. Augustine's influence is apparent here. Concupiscence is important for his understanding of sin. The wickedness of concupiscence is precisely that it constitutes a disordered love. Concupiscence drives people either to love the wrong things or to love the right things in the wrong way. In either case, one rebels against the command of God and perverts and harms God's good creation.

5. That is, in the abstract, in theory, in discussion.

about or is familiar with these and those wicked things. It is first unlike innocence in that the inclination to evil is right there next to cleverness, it only lies concealed and merely needs a provocation or opportunity, then it does not hesitate to spring forth; accordingly what was universal before the Fall is particular after the Fall and can be said only of a few persons and things. Only certain depravities are generally known to us. One person is by nature not unchaste, the second is not arrogant, the third not miserly, the fourth not lazy. But [this does not come about] out of love for the Savior but rather partly out of good parental up-bringing, partly because the structure of the substance of the soul itself moves certain people to set ideas in motion, but in others produces an incompetence. A person can therefore by nature be to some extent chaste, humble, generous or hard working and diligent, or at least appear to be, and in the process foster the vain hope that he is holy and a child of God.

One can little by little become accustomed to natural holiness also through the teaching of morals and manners, especially if one made a good beginning, and has undergone many misadventures. Then people also through reason and the coherence of their rules get used to thinking chastely, tenderly and lovingly, humbly, [and] compassionately. And that is distinguished from outward play-acting, where a person only displays virtuousness while the heart itself is full of deliberate viciousness and depravity.

But for all that the holiness that comes from reason is nothing because it is not acquired through the One who must work all things (Philippians 2:13). The children of reason are children of wrath (Ephesians 2:3). The happiness of the natural person consists in his obtaining his goal and maintaining the acquired thing as long as he wants. I will not speak of those who seek a happiness that is completely imagined or again is immediately just gone, but rather of those who have an appearance or image [of happiness] before them, for example a happy marriage, healthy and well trained children, an orderly and debt free household, a reasonable neighborhood, and moderate and meager freedom. But if a person has everything gathered together and the heart is not at home where it belongs, then neither one nor all have the power to keep human persons happy without the help of putting to sleep or deadening the deepest self.[6] That is also the reason why happiness after the Fall comes to nothing.

In the third place, now after the death of Jesus what are true wisdom, true righteousness, true holiness and redemption with the incomparable attribute of unwithering permanence? Wisdom is the simple and immoveable contemplation [of the truth] that the active love of Jesus is the highest and only knowledge, (deserving of the soul and its contemplation), that it is most unfortunate for a thought to move away from this great object, and that his death and suffering shall rest in our hearts until body and soul are separated. Righteousness is when a person's own righteousness, all that one has by either nature or reason, has fallen away, so that one allows witness to be given concerning the Savior and believes that our future claim depends upon mercy and grace, and we may desire all that Jesus has acquired for us all through his merit and when he poured out his blood for us on the wood of the cross. And that is an eternal righteousness that Jesus has devised. Whoever has it knows it. All imagination, what one thought one had and what one actually had was damned. But what he has now is grace. As long as a person still knows something with which one can help oneself besides the reconciliation, the blood and intercession of Jesus, one has to await nothing less than grace and mercy. Before we take our refuge with our whole heart in the little prayer, "Lord, have mercy," the Savior has no connection with us. All our goodness must first become sin to us, and all our power must become powerlessness.

Our innocence after the Fall begins with sanctification and merges into the old innocence. But no one who does not have the righteousness of Jesus is innocent. Since if a person is the same in one, then she is not in the other.[7] Whoever has acquired righteousness in the blood of Jesus receives power to tread underfoot and rule over everything wicked that he knows of himself concerning which one must always carefully seek and study, until finally when we remain with the Savior a long time, things altogether are forgotten, and one lives only in the Savior, which ultimately through enduring grace is brought [about] by the faithful

6. Zinzendorf means that under the conditions of finitude enduring human happiness is unattainable. The heart will always long for something. Only in God's eschatological kingdom will people know true and enduring happiness.

7. That is to say, insofar as one asserts one's own righteousness, one has none of Christ's. The only way to have his is to surrender one's own.

following of the Savior, as it says, "I live, but not I, rather Christ lives in me" (Galatians 2:20). Since insofar as one lives for oneself, one remains a sinner. A justified person allows himself to get mixed up with exactly nothing. One practices forever more in the opposite and what is roused one also overpowers. Whoever now begins to lose experience in evil through disuse becomes an innocent person in Christ.

Happiness is that we get back again and enjoy everything that we had before the Fall; good days, peace, contentment, all suitable to the purpose of happiness and progress, but in the spirit, in the heart. By all means, the body keeps its order, and children of God experience here exactly what he experienced when he was in the world. Our heart however is happy, secure, and certain. We are made masters over our bodies and its troubles and are always contented, even if to all appearance it is still so difficult. Now that is the fact.

But how does this come about? How do we become so wise, so righteous, so innocent and so happy and eternally so? The method by which to gain wisdom is the instruction and teaching of the Gospel. A doctrine grew up in the world that shows people the way. It is not composed of several thousand words that hang together, but rather when Jesus Christ teaches us then we experience words of excellence, words that one cannot express. We receive a godly assurance that it is so, that it is so constituted. The wisdom of this world is changeable, but this wisdom is unchangeable. It is precisely the wisdom that the apostles had. That is also our wisdom. The most wretched and the lowliest people who had Jesus in the most grim and ominous times spoke in the same way that we speak, although with different words. As long as the world exists no soul has come to be saved otherwise than by grace (without merit and without works) through the blood of Jesus Christ and his merit, by eternal predestination in Christ. Outside this grace, each one has one's own head for oneself alone, but here [within grace] we are all of one mind in Christ. This wisdom is the secret of the merit of Jesus Christ, of which souls know nothing on the basis of nature, and [of which they] can say nothing solid and definite, even if they still know how to say so many good things about everything else.

This wisdom must be given to us from above. We have no head for it by nature. No learned or bright person can make it up. No natural cleverness can conceive it. But as soon as the Savior begins to instruct, [this wisdom] is not demonstrated with numerous arguments and reasons, but rather he brings something into the heart that one feels and that constantly supports it. It is nothing but divine power and divine wisdom.

The way to gain righteousness that is thorough and eternal is justification. The Savior has one method with a view toward the whole human race and again another for each soul in particular. The method for the whole human race to acquire righteousness is this: "God said to his dear Son, The time of mercy is here; Go down [to earth] O most treasured crown of my heart! And be the salvation of the destitute and help them out of sin's affliction, put bitter death to death for them and make them to live with you."[8]

What became of this divine conclusion? "It was a strange war when death and life struggled. Life achieved the victory and swallowed up death."[9] How did it happen? "Scripture has borne witness how one death devoured the other. Meanwhile the true Easter Lamb, whom God required for us, is on the stem of the cross, roasted in the heat of passionate love; whose blood puts a sign on our door that faith looks upon as death, the murderer cannot strike us now."[10]

I use these simple rhymes, because in them it is so clear and plain that the blood of Jesus Christ, of the Son of God, is the cause of our righteousness. We cannot believe that. We must then first become fools with respect to our reason. We must learn well, or experience it, when we come under the Law through the grace of God. If we do not want to believe simply, then the Law applies to us and we must be tormented and harassed, so long until the Holy Spirit as it were gets compassion upon us and manifests the Savior deep in our hearts; and when we see there, (tired and weak, despondent over ourselves and over the whole world) then justification of the soul in particular takes place. "He presents them to his Father, that he has done enough for them [to be redeemed and accepted]."[11] Then the soul within becomes eternally privileged. [This soul] enters into eternal salvation through the blood of Jesus Christ, [and this blood] assuredly conducts one through the world and through sin and affliction, indeed through hell itself, and [the soul] can be hindered nowhere, from going into eternal happiness.

8. Again Zinzendorf quotes a hymn to make his point. It rhymes in German.
9. Another hymn quotation helps the Count express himself.
10. A hymn quotation.
11. For Zinzendorf this line from a hymn says it best.

Sanctification is that the Holy Spirit manifests to us in his light that everything we formerly understood as good and happy are in fact wretched, miserable things, satanic lusts, or imitations of the one good that we shall have in Jesus. If the Savior has only forgiven our old sins, then one permits trespass gladly to remain. The Holy Spirit assures us that our sins are forgiven through the name of Jesus, so that we may leave sinning behind and with that [the Holy Spirit] creates a completely different plan in the heart. For the arrogant person nothing is more abominable and repulsive than fame and honor; lust repels the lascivious; idleness terrifies the lazy; and the greedy make the cross as it were to oppose riches. The Savior leads this work forth from the first until the very last day of life. We continually become more godly, more righteous, and more happy. And the Savior does not make the ungodly to be good little by little, like some moral doctrines try to do, but rather it must all be renounced suddenly and all at once. The Savior washes asunder all wickedness with his blood and crushes it with his power and rips the whole system of sin to pieces.

But the good has its stages. The person becomes more chaste, more humble, more generous, more industrious or, in order to make myself still more clear, the student grows into an adult and by and by into a teacher. Fundamentally one always learns the secret of sanctification looking inward, always becomes accustomed to the routine of proper behavior in the practice of it, always becomes more and more able to follow through with it and to bring it to another; and after one is more and more improved in blessed contemplation, always exercises the practice more, after bringing the thing many times to another and through habit in all senses that are practiced and through an experience of hope; then one commends [this way] to others, thoroughly explains it to them, shows them also the routine of it and becomes for them a happy and blessed forerunner, until they themselves can also get to know the one who leads and takes care of us, the Holy Spirit, who is the Caretaker and Guardian of all souls.

Redemption as the means to make people blessed and happy, as that for which Jesus died on the cross, consists in this: that Jesus the crucified redeemed us from all causes of our wretchedness, from sin and the things that go with it, and [Jesus] teaches us to do and to put up with things for his sake. As [Jesus] began that once for the sake of the soul, so it goes on continually until the end. Blessedness or happiness is when nothing else delights a person except the Savior. And because we have the immoveable One with us, because nothing in the world is powerful [enough] to accomplish a separation between the Savior and us, his peace guards our hearts and minds forevermore; it is fine for us, wherever we go and stand, sit and lie, wake and sleep, triumph and suffer, live and die.

The world does not dare to hinder our happiness for very long. "The flesh must finally [get] out of the mind, as it always struggles so much." Malice alone is left over, the power of which is great and terrifying and makes itself so hardworking around believers, and strides as near to them as it more and more can, where it can have the smallest presumption to bring something to them; in consequence of which the Savior not only taught us to pray diligently and redeemed us from evil, but rather took it to be necessary to pray for us himself so that in the time when Satan desires to sift us, our faith does not fail.[12] But both the former and the latter and also the promise are founded on [the fact] that the Lord wanted to rescue his chosen ones in the near future, founded only on [the truth] that the Savior is the Redeemer for us.

---

12. Even our endurance, our persistence, in faith depends not on us, on our piety, on any of our efforts. It depends entirely on the Savior and on his prayer for us. All is in the Savior's hands.

The Fifteenth Speech
(8 April 1738)

Just as He Is Risen from the Dead, and Lives and Reigns Eternally

OUT OF THE CONTEXT ONE SEES THAT WHAT PRECEDED [I.E., THAT HE is risen and lives and reigns eternally] must be reiterated deep within the self: "We shall live under him in his kingdom, and serve him in eternal righteousness, innocence and happiness, just as he also is risen," etc. "I live and you shall live also" (John 14:9). That is the Savior's brief declaration.

We want to learn to believe two truths from this. First, [we want to learn] that he lives, and second, [we need to learn] that we shall also live. With respect to the first, that the Savior lives, we want to look upon the One who lives and upon the quality of his life. The divine truths may be taken only as they are expressed, in that way they are most clear. The One who lives is the One who lay in the grave, who tasted death for us all. The nature of the thing brought forth its [conclusion], the Son of God could not remain in death. If sons of great kings and princes do humble service, and take vulgar, inferior circumstances upon themselves, still everyone knows, and the conclusion is easily drawn, that [baseness] is not the state of affairs in which they remain, and is not their own, but rather when it is serious, then [this humble service] is certainly intended for something that is worth the effort. Whoever has seen the Son of God in his lowliness and suffering unto death and has thereby believed that he is in truth the Son of God, such a [believing] person must necessarily have concluded from it that [the Savior] does not remain thus [bowed down with suffering], but rather, that something inexpressibly great will arise from his suffering.

Therefore the Lord scolds the disciples and bears witness to them (Luke 24:25), that they proceed without connection and consequence, as fools and phlegmatic heads. They believed that he is the Son of God, and when Peter said, "You are the Christ, Son of the living God," Jesus answered, "Flesh and blood has not revealed this to you, but rather my Father in heaven" (Matthew 16:16–17). The Son of God made arrangements for eternally abiding life for so many souls. The way was his death. No soul goes into eternity, before the throne of God, unless its hut is transformed; for that very reason the Savior laid his body in the grave in the place where the others are laid down. But because he had not time and did not need to remain longer in death, he rose again through the power of God in a few days. By his resurrection he made a multitude of many familiar friends part of his resurrection. He even took several people and made them like himself, and did not let them see the vessel of decay, because he did not want to possess some human perfection without permitting at least one or another of his brothers to become like him in it. Therefore he led the two witnesses (Luke 9:30)[1] out of the world so quickly, before death was so to speak over and done. Indeed, he did more to them. He was like them only in that he did not see corruption; but he endured his full portion of death, which he spared them.

He experienced many thousand afflictions, and they were ultimately loosed through his power. Since he has the key to death. Just as he took action as Lord in his death, so he also did the same in the grave. He remained in it as long as he wanted, the length of time he determined. He left the grave in accordance with his good judgment, after the offering of his body, and after that he went around among those who belonged to him as long as he thought necessary. Who is the One who lives? It is the eternal Son of God in the bosom of the Father, before whom all creatures in heaven must bow and every tongue confess that he is the Lord, to the glory of God the Father (Philippians 2:10–11).

But what is the quality of his life? The true start of our life is to be sought, as everyone knows, in what people call death. The beginning of

---

1. The two witnesses in the passage are Moses and Elijah. In Scripture Elijah was taken up in a chariot (2 Kings 2:11), and Moses died alone with God and God buried him in an unknown place (Deuteronomy 34:5–6).

natural life is a sealing up of the soul within a dying body, but the end is the liberation of [the soul], and then for the first time the life of the soul begins.[2] Human life is a continual dying. When the Savior says, then, "I live," it does not mean that he remains with them in the flesh and wanted to drag along eternally under the sicknesses that he bore, but rather that he goes to his Father to live without end and that he himself wanted to begin to draw human souls to himself.

The disciples of course did not understand this. They conceived of the Messiah according to the past and also prevailing idea of the Jews, as a worldly Lord. But if they had experienced it as they experienced it afterwards, then their delight was very great. "You would rejoice because I go away" (John 14:28). The life of which the Savior speaks consists in that he showed himself alive after his death, and lives and reigns in eternity. "Christ, awakened from the dead, dies henceforth nevermore" (Romans 6:9). He lives forevermore and prays for us (Hebrews 7:25). He conquered and has seated himself upon his Father's throne (Revelation 3:21). That is the Savior's mode of life. He works continually so that the world endures, and that is his ancient divine work. But he works also as human and always draws one after another and intercedes for them to his Father. And he looks toward his enemies, pursues them and preserves them, until he must permit now and then, here and there, an example to them for the good of the world.

The life continues from eternity to eternity according to the special word, "The servant does not remain eternally in the house, but the Son remains eternally" (John 8:35). Or as it is expressed in the epistle to the Hebrews, "He establishes the Son, perfect forever" (Hebrews 7:28), that is, the time of his service, of his subordination, is so magnificent, [though] at the same time to be sure the Father's throne is higher, [but this subordination] will have an end when all his enemies themselves are brought under him and the bearers of the charge will have carried out the great commission. And that is the life of our Savior.

Now it says, secondly, "You shall live." The Savior spoke here of us and of our life. We are the persons who shall live. It is nothing bad to live and indeed to live like Jesus and with Jesus to sit upon the throne of his Father. I consider everything to be loss compared with the extravagant

---

2. Zinzendorf here expresses a Platonic view of the soul. The biblical way of thinking is actually quite different in important respects. He seems not to have thought much about this. The most pressing and urgent problems in his day lay elsewhere.

knowledge of Jesus Christ, my Lord, for whose sake I count everything as loss and consider it to be filth[3] so that I might win Christ and be found in him" (Philippians 3:8–9). He wanted only to have that alone and to move towards the resurrection of the dead. He wanted to know that it is certain that he may live and that he was not afraid of his own [death] anymore.

Not all people will live to him. "You will die in your sins," says the Savior to a crowd of people (John 8:24). When you have brought your life out of this world in the end, which is nothing other than death, and [have done it] either with a philosophical idea that after death will be another, better, life, or with a delusional faith and imaginary hope of salvation, or believing exactly nothing, [when you] lay aside the hut of this death that had entangled your souls, then you will come up against a new death and you will die. The reasons why people die the second death are well known, "Because," says the Holy Spirit, "They do not believe in the name of the only begotten Son of God" (John 3:18). I want to give a brief specification of those who die the second death and go into the pool that burns with fire and brimstone, which is the second death (Revelation 21:8). One does not have to be a murderer, a prostitute, or a thief, etc. If one has only one single quality, which I will now name as I find it in the pleasant apostle John, one dies the eternal death with certainty.

The despondent or despairing belong in the pool. To be in despair means perhaps always to begin and to resolve anew that one wants to be converted, but abandoning it over and over sometimes for this reason, sometimes for that. I do not describe malicious sinners, but rather those who die over their desires (Proverbs 21:25). Those who do not take hold of the power of the death of Jesus Christ, and who therefore also fail to apprehend the glory of his life, still can say truly, "I am his. I am his own possession and want to live under him in his kingdom and serve him in eternal righteousness, innocence and happiness." Whoever cannot say that is a terribly unhappy person and dies the second death, when he dies here in time.

Our thoughts about ourselves can easily deceive us, more is necessary for that purpose, a determination belongs to it, a word, a faith, if we do not want to die eternally. One must conceive the resurrection as if it

---

3. Zinzendorf follows Luther's translation and uses the word *Dreck* here. It means "filth," or "mire." It is also used as a term for "dung."

were already there, direct one's heart toward the heights and go toward the resurrection. That means being steady and solid, not wavering, not retreating, but rather holding to the resurrected Jesus whom one does not see as if one saw him.

Thus the one who believes is the one who lives, who rejoices over nothing except the Savior and his resurrection and who does not rest or gently lay down his head until he knows this with certainty, "Indeed, Amen [truly], I will live."

The Savior sometimes sets up a trial for his children and allows them to scrutinize how they stand. But all hesitations and doubtfulness that the Savior sends us if we are his, only serve that we may find even more reason to rejoice. Our wretchedness and weakness cannot keep us back. Whoever is once with the Savior does not have to retreat from him, even when something is there such that one dares not to come before the high and majestic Creator. Precisely then one says to the Crucified, to the Savior who was brought so low, "Here I have something that I cannot bring before your throne. Help me out of my poverty. Take it away. Wash it away. And where it does not go away, then sit and melt it" (Malachi 3:3); "And choose me in the furnace of affliction" (Isaiah 48:10).

Whoever only does not despair can be free every hour and every instant from all that torments him, from all trials and condemnations. The poor, miserable sinners whom Jesus sought and found certainly live, but had no peace until they were pardoned.[4] And that it is not unjust when the despairing are lost is [also] very clear from this: there is almost no example of a person who is intent on acquiring the hope, giving up even if they had the worst chimera as an object until the soul leaves the body, and on the other hand one sees many thousands who are given peace in good time with respect to their eternal welfare and grief, from mistrust, from the wicked, abominable blasphemy, as the dear *Catechism* rightly names it, and [peace] from despair and doubt in the good will of the One, "Who simply gives to everyone and puts it on top of no one" (James 1:5), and to whom each human soul became so bitter to redeem, and therefore [each one] is just as costly and dear as the other.

---

4. The term I have translated as "pardoned" means literally "begraced." His point is that until you have been begraced, you do not have power over despair, and therefore you do not have the power to live in true liberty and joy.

But what concerns the life that we receive continues in two parts. The first is: we died, and our life is hidden with Christ in God (Colossians 3:3). The second is: "But when Christ, who is our life, is revealed, then we shall also be revealed with him in glory." We live from the moment when Jesus said to us, "You shall live" (Ezekiel 16:6). The Savior awakens not only whole peoples and lands, [and] one clearly sees that such a general awakening has its times and hours, when one can say that the house, the city or the whole country has a year of grace, salvation befalls them, but also each individual soul in particular. If the soul is only qualified for grace, if he only sees, if the soul will accept the call of grace, it may be as a rule as it wills. Thus, [the Savior] draws the soul. Thus he calls it. This happens to one person now, to another at a different time, and if it does not happen then that is also kind heartedness because the same person whom [the Savior] does not win over were he to make his appeal a thousand times, grace assuredly does not protect, and therefore [that soul] would be doubly damned. For that reason he sometimes permits souls with no engagement of the heart to go away from the preaching of the Gospel. But whomever the Savior awakens is a happy person indeed. Then it is very probably at hand that it can become something enduring. Then one must prepare oneself to act with the matter and seriously make it one's business, and for the sake of the matter let everything pass by, and in ideas be captivated with nothing that does not deal with what is now our same sole means to salvation.

The beginning of spiritual life is truly an undeniable anxiety or unease, an agitation or disquiet, that is not ended until one is born of God, until a person (according to the Savior's expression, John 16:21) is born into the world. Because the spiritual joy, and the Holy Communion of the Lord with the soul, is the intimation that a child is there, because it gets food and drink. One cannot promise souls that their coming to life will finish without all grief and days of pain. But it is also not necessary that the heart should be confused over this, but rather one goes peacefully among these sufferings. And whoever is so wise that he instantly flings away with a single word everything [of the old life], all the pleasures, thoughts, fantasies and splendors of the world, and reflects on what kind of life Jesus had, full of joy, delight and peace (though all in the heart, of course); is soon helped out of death into life on the other side, into grace, peace, forgiveness, life and happiness.

The hidden life in God, the happiness in Christ, begins from the instant when we know what we have in the Savior. People think we are lost, an organized community of the dead. We are now made good for nothing and miserable, but [in truth] we have become citizens with the elect and members of God's household. With respect to the superficial and publicly visible sign [of our status], we often do nothing different from what the other [unbelieving] people do, but with a childlike, loving and joyful heart in relation to God and other people. That is shapeless and unrecognized in the eyes of others, a hidden life. But the Eye that sees into every nook and cranny see this life. "The daughter of the king is wholly glorious within" (Psalm 45:14). "The hidden person of the heart in gentle and quiet spirit is very precious before God" (1 Peter 3:4). Within the heart it is just as it is in heaven.

How will it now appear in our Father's kingdom? There is not much to say about that. Our speeches only have the aim of awakening the mind to think further about the matter and to enter into the word of God, that word [that is] to be sure better than all human words, if one reads it just as it is written with a heart that is moved and set in motion, that is awakened to life.[5] This refers to the Lamb. The word also bears witness to the Lamb, but with an expression that we do not know how to make up even with our best understanding, with a near and deeply inward feeling of the heart that must first be brought about by our speeches.[6]

I commend to you all these words for mature and heartfelt consideration. Allow the Holy Spirit to preach in your heart that Jesus lives and that you also shall live.

---

5. For the Count, a proper Christian reading of Scripture can only take place through the power of the Holy Spirit. God must work in a person's reading. The Holy Spirit must enlighten the mind and kindle fire in the heart. Only God can make these weak and stumbling human words, which after all the words of Scripture are also, to be God's own Word.

6. So the aim of Zinzendorf's speeches is not merely to impart information. But rather, it is to be a part of the Lord's bringing about a "deeply inward feeling of the heart."

The Sixteenth Speech
(9 April 1738)

This Is Most Certainly True

THIS IS THE LAST WORD OF THE EXPLICATION OF THE SECOND ARTICLE [of the creed]. "I know in whom I believe, and am certain, that he can guard what is entrusted to me until the Last Day" (2 Timothy 1:12).

I believe that my Savior, my king, bears his name with honor.

I believe his eternal deity.

I believe his true and authentic humanity.

I believe that I am one of his servants.

I believe that I was lost. I knew the judgment of death against me. But I believe with complete certainty that I am ransomed and absolved.

I believe that I am the rightful and legitimate wage for all his work, all of his toil and his sweat.

I believe that he fought for me and won me with his sword and bow.

I believe that I am no longer guilty or reckoned as sinful [before God].

I believe that I will not die.

I believe that I am now master over the devil.

I believe that I am redeemed neither by word or work, nor by miracle, nor by the absolute command of God, nor through a new creation, nor by any other means, but rather through the death penalty that the Son of God endured for me.

I believe that I now belong to no one except the One who earned me.

I believe that he reigns over all in kingly power.

I believe that I live under him where I am, under his protection, under his peace and under his order. I am certain that I have the unshakeable privilege that all my fellow citizens [in the household of God] have, that I am as immovably godly as they are [and] that I am as unceasingly happy as they all are.

But I also believe that without him I am nothing and that I live only by virtue of this: that he lives. So long as he lives, I also live.

And I know all this as certainly as I know that my head stands between my shoulders. [And I also know] that it is a great necessity that each person should be able to confess, "I believe." One sees this in the question the Savior asked many times, "Do you believe?" "If only you could believe!" "Can you believe?" He asked this even before he revealed his glory and majesty, when he had after all immediately decided to perform wonders. And without faith it is impossible to please God. Whoever wants to come to God must believe that he is and that he will be the Rewarder of those who seek him (Hebrews 11:6).

Faith is the great duty of all duties. What the simultaneously received law imposes upon a person as an obligation, in order that one may recognize the poverty and corruption of one's heart in foolish revolt against one's great happiness, is now called a blessing according to the Gospel and belongs in a completely different chapter. "I will make a new covenant with them, not as the covenant that I made with their ancestors, when I took them by the hand so that I might lead them out of Egypt, which covenant they have not kept and I had to force them, said the Lord. No more call it the Lord's burden" (Jeremiah 31:31–32). "I will give my law into their hearts and write it within them, and they shall be my people and I will be their God" (Jeremiah 31:33). The will of God should be food and drink for people (John 4:34). These are all true Christian things, to show loyalty, to practice love, to do from the heart everything one does. That is their life, and if they can make progress soundly in this, it is good for them.

Their sole unhappiness is that they sometimes do not know rightly how to find themselves, they have insufficient understanding, no experience, no fortitude to do what they gladly want to do. But because all that is not a duty, and in the New Testament it no longer says, "You shall be humble, you shall be chaste, you shall be generous, you shall be hardworking," but rather "I am redeemed through the blood of the Son of God from pride, from lust, from covetousness, and from sloth, I may be humble, I may be chaste, I may be contented, I may be hardwork-ing, it is permitted to me, and the blood of Jesus has accomplished this for me," thus one does not have to be troubled about anything except about faith.

Faith can be considered in two ways.

1) According to its cause, which Luther calls a divine work in the soul that changes us and gives us new birth from God (John 1:13), and kills the old Adam and makes us into completely different people from the heart, spirit, mind and all [our] powers and brings with it the Holy Spirit. This divine work of bringing forth, besides belongs to nothing other than the ordinary process of God's economy of salvation, that Scripture calls "faith," or the work of faith in power.

2) According to its effect, by which something is that is our own, that is called "believing." One hears the word of reconciliation and it agitates and prevails upon our hearts until our believing blends with the Gospel (Hebrews 4:2) and our hearts think the same way as the Gospel (cf. Genesis 45:26). If now we forevermore continue to believe in this way, and our hearts are one with it and think exactly as it stands, "What God promised, he is able also to do," then we get something in us that we did not have before. We experience the glory of the cross to our astonishment. Our hearts, minds, desires, notions, emotions and fortitude are changed. Not only must others admit that it is a miracle that a person is as she is, but rather we are astonished at ourselves, I say, we become a marvel to ourselves, because we see with [newly] seeing eyes that he has given us of his Spirit.

Who does not see that we must know certainly, we believe, if we want to have a part in godly and heavenly things? When the Savior also undertakes something extraordinary and takes hold of a person in the midst of sins, in the middle of godless dealings (which he can do, he does it many times; though to be sure no one can count on it happen-ing to him or her) then at the same time faith is also there. We see that in Paul. In the moment when Jesus had mercy on him, when God willed to reveal his Son to him, when he was allowed to hear the voice, immediately he exclaimed, "Lord!" he said, "Who are you?" (Acts 9:4; Galatians 1:16–17). Scarcely had Jesus made himself known, when the persecutor of the Church believed, the man who the minute before had intended to do much wickedness to the name of Jesus, [now believed] in the name. "What do you want me to do, Lord?" he said. "Only enter into the city. There you shall hear." What came after that? It was said to him in confidence how much good he shall be granted to get, but nothing more than that.

Certainly the Savior asks accordingly nothing. Just as we are in the hour when he has mercy upon us, when he gives us grace, let us be as we will, still he gives us grace and forgives us our sins. But the moment when that happens he makes us other than we were. The blood of Christ, that represents us before the Father, has its effect immediately by making us pure and sanctifying us. When one sees no change in the person, then one can truthfully say, "Either you have not received grace, or you have forgotten the purification of your sins," which is as much as to forget his salvation. As soon as one gets grace one automatically shuns the vanities of the world, and allows the work of the Savior to make progress in one's heart with inward love, one does not allow to well up that which still for our humiliation remains there, for the remembrance of the ruin, and this is not to be looked at as a weakness, but rather it is to be seen as sinful, one never permits it to come to power, it must be subordinated, because we are now able to do what we will. That is what happens with faith.

But one must also know in whom one believes. The souls that the Savior has drawn to himself and to whom he now gives grace do not always have exactly the most distinct concepts of the One in whom they should believe. The man born blind demonstrates this (John 9:36). "Lord, who is it, so that I may believe in him?" They know that they have been snatched out of their wretchedness and love the One who is merciful to them. But they often study a long time over it before they learn to know him properly, namely, who he is. The fathers in Christ claimed that they know him who was from the beginning (1 John 2:13). To know the Savior in all his lowliness, in all his glory, is the greatest happiness. Jesus must never be seen otherwise than on the cross, in his blood, and in his abasement, if our hearts are to be contented. Paul knows nothing except Jesus Christ crucified, and, to be sure, on the cross (1 Corinthians 2:2). We remember in our hearts, that he also now sits at the right hand of God and is the Lord upon the throne of the whole world. But if we insist upon his exaltation alone, and forget who he already was before the world was made, then it only makes half an impression and the ordination is far from the condition, as if we say to each other in circular form and say again and again, that God, who paled on the cross, made us along with all creatures.

To know in whom one believes means to see Jesus, who is in the bosom of God his Father, in the spirit of the crucifixion of his deepest self, with spiritual eyes to behold and touch the nail holes. It is a different thing to preach about it, to set forth reasons, to be able to explain it clearly; those are gifts that are to be taken along already, if they are available according to the mind of God and bear some resemblance to faith, but it is not an essential part of faith.

A person who has the poorest mind can often believe much more solidly than the most learned and clever person. "Faith is not everyone's thing" (2 Thessalonians 3:2). [Faith itself] is a grace and a mercy. It is given to us to believe in the name of the only begotten Son of God. That is the reason why it is certainly a false idea, as if we, when we wanted to believe the Gospel, had to be people weak in understanding and have only half a brain. We have to believe much that we do not see in the world, since [whether we have] well being and pain often depends on things we do not see. That one finds it so hard to believe in the thing of the Savior does not come from the difficulty of the matter, but rather from corrupted nature. Therefore, we must all be ashamed that we do not believe, that we do not know rightly in whom we believe, and must allow faith to be given or strengthened, given if we do not yet have it, strengthened if we do not have the fullness of salvation, if the Savior has not yet become as tangible to us, in [both] his lowliness and grandeur, as our nature could nevertheless bear.

I must also know in whom I believe. He is God. He has all the treasures of eternity and can do all things. He is human. I can keep company with him in a childlike manner, even if I am still so wretched, so miserable and poor, and can only think and pray from the heart, "Have mercy on me, show yourself to me, you who are my God and my Savior." These two notions have together in a glance what it means to know in whom one believes.[1]

Third, one must know that it will remain thus. I am certain that he can preserve what is laid by for me until the last day (2 Timothy 1:12). A "laid by thing" means a thing that is already put away for one, that

---

1. So for the Count, knowing God is dependent first upon God's initiative and action. Then, faith must follow. This produces of itself a life of discipleship, which in turn causes one to perceive, understand, and know in a new way and with a new depth.

one shall receive it at its time. "As long as the heir is a child there is no distinction between him and a servant, although he is a master of all the goods; but rather he is under the guardians and trustees until the time appointed by the father" (Galatians 4:1–2). So it is with us. We do not yet enjoy it. We are not yet with him, in the meantime it is set aside for us, saved, etc. it does not first have to be created and made, but rather only made visible and given. One can say: "My inheritance is in heaven, my crown, my blessing, my happiness abides for me. I will without doubt find it, no matter how things go for me here in time, in this mortal life. It is completely certain that my portion and inheritance is prepared for me, even when I fall and die, then my heaven sinks not."[2]

That sounds almost as if a person who once has faith can never again lose it. And to be sure if one does not want to lose it one does not have to. But whoever wants to can, like a dog, forget his cleansing, or like a sow he can be twisted up in the filth of the world again (2 Peter 2:22), that is also true. Already in the time of the apostles several turned back to Satan again (1 Timothy 5:15).

You may ask, "Why is this freedom permitted to us?" First, for reasons that I do not know and that do not even enter into human thoughts, but which are incomparably good and well grounded. Second, because Eternal Love has not built heaven as a cage for souls, nor as a prison, but rather as a collecting place of all those for whom his love is [intended] for happiness, peace and freedom. To love him and to attach oneself to him is a very wise thing to do. It is due to the fact that our free choice and the spontaneity of our love help with our preservation.

We can remain if we want to do it. But by all means our true security is to be sought in his faithfulness. Nothing can tear us out of his hand. (John 10:28) The devil, the world, our flesh and blood, sin itself can take nothing from us. We do this ourselves by a free and unchained will if we depart. And in Hebrews 6:6 the apostle calls that "crucifying the Son of God anew," and also in 10:29 [he says such a person], "tramples the Son of God underfoot, treats the blood of the covenant as an unimportant thing, and insults the Spirit of grace." And the sayings about such people are dreadful. Therefore each soul should daily and hourly ask, indeed with worry, "Do you still remain in faith?"

The apostle calls this to contend for the faith, (Jude v. 3) to look around constantly at whether there is something mistaken in us that

---

2. This is a hymn text.

could take faith [away] from us. The Savior says in John 6:67, "Do you want to go away?" just as he formerly said, "Do you want to come?" Happy is the person who answers with Peter, "Lord, where shall I go? You have the words of eternal life."

Whoever is born of God does not sin, because his seed abides in her and cannot sin, since she is born of God (1 John 3:9). She is protected (1 John 5:18). Before the forgiveness of sins comes no one can be preserved. One can neither be roused nor moved in spiritual goods. One can otherwise do many things. One can perform miracles of faith, move mountains and defend nations through faith. All [these deeds] prove nothing; indeed even martyrdom proves nothing, if faith and love are not together in the heart. They both have to be there. In Scripture they are often thrown together, because they coalesce the same instant that faith comes to be and one has forgiveness of sins. From that hour on one lives and works in love. Then a person can do good and not grow tired. "If you are now raised with Christ, then seek what is above, where Christ is, seated at the right hand of God" (Colossians 3: 1). "Whoever has such hope purifies himself as [God] also is pure" (1 John 3:3).

Now we have talked through the second article of our Christian faith. I set my seal on it with my whole heart. I joyfully subscribe to this: that God is real and that my Reconciler is everything to me. God wills that all the people say, "Amen!"

Bibliography

1. Works Cited

Augustine. "The Enchiridion." In *Saint Augustine: On the Holy Trinity, Doctrinal Treatises, Moral Treatises*, edited by Philip Schaff, 237–76. Translated by J. F. Shaw. The Nicene and Post-Nicene Fathers, first ser. 3. Grand Rapids: Eerdmans, 1980.

Aulen, Gustaf. *Christus Victor*. Translated by A. G. Herbert. New York: Macmillan, 1969. Reprint, Eugene, OR: Wipf & Stock, 2003.

Herbert of Cherbury, Edward Herbert. *De Veritate*. Translated with an introduction by Meyrick H. Carré. Bristol Studies 6. Bristol UK: Arrowsmith, 1937.

Luther, Martin. *Studienausgabe*. Volume 1, *Von der Freiheit eines Christenmenschen*. Edited by Otto Clemen. Luthers Werke. Berlin: de Gruyter, 1967.

Placher, William. *The Domestication of Transcendence*. Louisville: Westminster John Knox, 1996.

Russell, William R. *Luther's Theological Testament: The Schmalkald Articles*. Minneapolis: Fortress, 1995.

Tappert, Theodore G., translator and editor. *The Book of Concord: The Confessions of the Evangelical Lutheran Church*. Philadelphia: Fortress, 1959.

2. Works by Count Zinzendorf

Zinzendorf, N. L. *Des Ordinarii Fratrum Berlinische Reden, nach dem vollständigen und von ihm selbst eigenhändig revidirten Exemplar*. Barby: Gottfried Clemens, 1758.

———. *Ergänzungsbände zu den Hauptschriften*. Edited by Erich Beyreuther and Gerhard Meyer. 14 vols. Hildesheim: Olms, 1964–1985.

———. *Gedanken über verschiedene evangelische Wahrheiten, aus dessen Schriften zusammengezogen*. Gnadau: verlag der Buchhandlung der Evangelischen Büder-Unität, 1840.

———. *Hauptschriften*. Edited by Erich Beyeuther and Gerhard Meyer. 6 vols. Hildesheim: Olms, 1962–1963.

———. *Maxims, Theological Ideas and Sentences, out of the Present Ordinary of the Brethren's Churches, His Dissertations and Discourses from the Years 1738–1747*. Extracted by J. Gambold. London: Beecroft, 1751.

————. *Nine Public Lectures on Important Subjects in Religion Preached in Fetter Lane Chapel in London in the Year 1746.* 1973. Translated and edited by George W. Forell. Reprint, Eugene, OR: Wipf & Stock. 1998.

3. Recommended Literature Related to Zinzendorf

Aalen, Leiv. *Die Theologie des jungen Zinzendorf.* Arbeiten zur Geschichte und Theologie des Luthertums 16. Berlin: Lutherisches, 1966.

Aland, Kurt, editor. *Pietismus und Bibel.* Arbeiten zur Geschichte des Pietismus 9. Witten: Luther, 1970.

Atwood, Craig. *Community of the Cross: Moravian Piety in Colonial Bethlehem.* University Park: Pennsylvania State University Press, 2004.

Baumgart, Peter. *Zinzendorf als Wegbereiter historischen Denkens.* Historische Studien 381. Lübeck: Matthiesen, 1960.

Becker, Bernhard. *Zinzendorf und sein Christentum im Verhältnis zum kirchlichen und religiösen Leben seiner Zeit.* Leipzig: Jansa, 1900.

Betterman, Wilhelm. *Theologie und Sprache bei Zinzendorf.* Gotha: Klotz, 1935.

Beyreuther, Erich. *Die junge Zinzendorf.* Marburg: Francke-Buchhandlung, 1957.

————. *Frömmigkeit und Theologie: Gesammelte Aufätze zum Pietismus und Erweckungsbewegung.* Hildesheim: Olms, 1980.

————. *Geschichte des Pietismus.* Stuttgart: Steinkopf, 1978.

————. *Nikolaus Ludwig von Zinzendorf in Selbstzeugnissen und Bilddokumenten.* Rowohlts Monographien 105. Reinbek: Rowohlt Taschenbuch, 1965.

————. *Studien zur Theologie Zinzendorfs.* Neukirchen-Vluyn: Neukirchener, 1962.

————. *Zinzendorf und die Christenheit, 1732–1760.* Marburg: Francke, 1961.

Brecht, Martin, and Klaus Deppermann, editors. *Geschichte des Pietismus.* Volume 2, *Der Pietismus im achtzehnten Jahrhundert.* Göttingen: Vandenhoeck & Ruprecht, 1995.

Campbell, Ted. *Religion of the Heart: A Study of European Religious Life in the Seventeenth and Eighteenth Centuries.* Columbia: University of South Carolina Press, 1991.

Clarke, W. K. Lowther. *Eighteenth Century Piety.* London: SPCK, 1944.

Creed, John Martin, and John Sandwith Boys Smith. *Religious Thought in the Eighteenth Century.* Cambridge: Cambridge University Press, 1934.

Deghaye, Pierre. *La Doctrine ésotérique de Zinzendorf.* Paris: Klincksieck, 1969.

Eberhard, Samuel. *Kreuzes-Theologie: Das reformatorische Anliegen in Zinzendorfs Verkündigen.* Munich: Kaiser, 1937.

Freeman, Arthur J. "The Hermeneutics of Count Nicolaus Ludwig von Zinzendorf." ThD diss., Princeton Theological Seminary, 1962.

————. *An Ecumenical Theology of the Heart: The Theology of Count Nicholas Ludwig von Zinzendorf.* Bethlehem, PA: Moravian Church in America, 1998.

Hirzel, Stephen. *Der Graf und die Brüder: die Geschichte einer Gemeinschaft.* Gotha: Klotz, 1935.

Hök, Gösta. *Zinzendorfs Begriff der Religion.* Uppsala Universitets Årsskrift 1948: 6. Leipzig: Harrassowitz, 1948.

Kinkel, Gary S. *It Started with Zinzendorf.* Moravian Church in Great Britain, 2000.

————. *Our Dear Mother the Spirit: An Investigation of Count Zinzendorf's Theology and Praxis.* Lanham, MD: University Press of America, 1990.

Lehmann, Hugo. *Zinzendorfs Religiosität.* Leipzig: Jansa, 1903.

Leube, Hans. *Orthodoxie und Pietismus: Gesammelte Studien.* Arbeiten zur Geschichte des Pietismus 13. Bielefeld: Luther, 1975.

Lewis, A. J. *Zinzendorf, the Ecumenical Pioneer: A Study in the Moravian Contribution to Christian Mission and Unity.* Christian Lives. Philadelphia: Westminster, 1962.

Lindberg, Carter, editor. *The Pietist Theologians: An Introduction to Theology in the Seventeenth and Eighteenth Centuries.* The Great Theologians. Malden, MA: Blackwell, 2005.

Mälzer, Gottfried. *Bengel und Zinzendorf: Zur Biographie und Theologie Albrecht Bengels.* Arbeiten zur Geschichte des Pietismus 3. Witten: Luther, 1968.

Mau, Joan. "Zinzendorf and the Augsburg Confession." MA thesis, University of Iowa School of Religion, 1976.

Meyer, Dieter. *Christozentrismus des späten Zinzendorf: Eine Studie zu dem Begriff "täglicher Umgang mit dem Heiland."* Europäische Hochschulschriften. Reihe 23, Theologie 25. Frankfurt: Lang, 1973.

Meyer, Dietrich, et al., editors. *Graf ohne Grenzen: Leben und Werk von Nikolaus Ludwig Graf von Zinzendorf.* Herrnhut: Unitätsarchiv in Herrnhut im Verlag der Comeniusbuchhandlung, 2000.

Meyer, Henry. *Child Nature and Nurture according to Nicolaus Ludwig von Zinzendorf.* Chicago: Abingdon, 1928.

Nielsen, Sigurd. *Intoleranz und Toleranz bey Zinzendorf.* Hamburg: Appel, n.d.

Plitt, Hermann. *Zinzendorf's Theologie.* 3 volumes. Gotha: Perthes, 1869–1874.

Rendtorff, Trutz, editor. *Religion als Problem der Aufklärung.* Göttingen: Vandenhoeck & Ruprecht, 1980.

Ritschl, Albrecht. *Die Geschichte des Pietismus.* 3 vols. Bonn: Marcus, 1880–1886.

Ruh, Hans. *Die christologische Begründung des ersten Artikels bei Zinzendorf.* Zürich: EVZ, 1967.

Schmidt, Martin. *Der Pietismus als theologische Erscheinung: Gesammelte Studien zur Geschichte des Pietismus.* Arbeiten zur Geschichte des Pietismus 20. Göttingen: Vandenhoeck & Ruprecht, 1984.

Schmidt, Martin, and Wilhelm Jannasch, editors. *Das Zeitalter des Pietismus.* Klassiker des Protestantismus 6. Bremen: Schünemann, 1965.

Smith, Peter. *European Thought in the Eighteenth Century.* Gloucester, UK: Smith, 1973.

Söhngen, Oskar, editor. *Die bleibende Bedeutung des Pietismus.* Witten: von Cansteinsche Bibelanstalt, 1960.

Stoeffler, F. Ernest. *German Pietism during the Eighteenth Century.* Studies in the History of Religions; Supplements to Numen 24. Leiden: Brill, 1973.

————. *The Rise of Evangelical Pietism.* Studies in the History of Religions 9. Leiden: Brill, 1965.

Uttendörfer, Otto. *Der Ursprung der Pädagogik Zinzendorfs und der Brüdergemeine.* Herrnhut: Missionsbuchhandlung, 1922.

————. *Nikolaus Ludwig Graf von Zinzendorf: Evangelische Gedanken.* Berlin: Christlicher Zeitschriftenverlag, 1948.

138 *Bibliography*

———. *Zinzendorfs christliches Lebensideal.* Gnadau: Unitätsbuchhandlung, 1940.
———. *Zinzendorf und die Mystik.* Berlin: Christlicher Zeitschriftenverlag, 1951.
———. *Zinzendorfs religiöse Grundgedanken.* Herrnhut: Missionsbuchhandlung, 1935.
Weinlick, John R. *Count Zinzendorf.* New York: Abingdon, 1956.
Zimmerling, Peter. *Gott in Gemeinschaft: Zinzendorfs Trinitätslehre.* Monographien und Studienbücher. Giessen: Brunnen, 1991.